The Next Buddha may be a Community

The Next Buddha may be a Community:
Practising Intercultural Competence
at Macquarie University, Sydney, Australia

By

Sabine Krajewski

CAMBRIDGE
SCHOLARS
PUBLISHING

The Next Buddha may be a Community:
Practising Intercultural Competence at Macquarie University, Sydney, Australia,
By Sabine Krajewski

This book first published 2011

Cambridge Scholars Publishing

12 Back Chapman Street, Newcastle upon Tyne, NE6 2XX, UK

British Library Cataloguing in Publication Data
A catalogue record for this book is available from the British Library

ISBN (10): 1-4438-3011-9, ISBN (13): 978-1-4438-3011-9

For Miglio.
For my friends.

"The Buddha, Shakyamuni, our teacher, predicted that the next Buddha would be Maitreya, the Buddha of love.... It is possible that the next Buddha will not take the form of an individual. The next Buddha may take the form of a community, a community practicing understanding and loving kindness, a community practicing mindful living. And the practice can be carried out as a group, as a city, as a nation."

—Thich Nhat Hanh, "The Next Buddha May Be A Sangha" in *Inquiring Mind*, Vol 10, No. 2, Spring 1994.

TABLE OF CONTENTS

LIST OF FIGURES

LIST OF TABLES

Chapter Two: A Delphi Study about Intercultural Competence at Macquarie University

Chapter Three: The Student Voice

PREFACE

When I joined Macquarie University in 2008 I was delighted to be teaching a postgraduate unit in Intercultural Communication with students from all over the planet. Each class typically comprises roughly 50% Asian students, mainly from mainland China but also from Hong Kong, Taiwan, Malaysia, South Korea, Japan, Indonesia, Thailand and India. Others are from Latin America (Brazil, Chile, Mexico, Argentina), Europe (France, Spain, Germany, Denmark, the Netherlands, Finland, UK), the US, Canada, and Australia. The university is located in Sydney, Australia's most multicultural city.

It is exciting to work with such diverse groups and most of the participants use the opportunity to share their previous knowledge and experience in other countries and to learn from each other. Nevertheless, my own research about the use and effect of experiential intercultural learning with student groups from this particular class across several semesters (Krajewski, 2011) has shown that in some cases stereotypes seem to be confirmed and students leave the class with an image of "the other" that is even more fixed. It revealed that some students find it very challenging to interact with someone from a different cultural and linguistic background and experience self-directed tasks in teams from different linguistic and cultural backgrounds as more difficult than they expected. At times, even students who consider themselves as very open towards such experiences and who crave opportunities to truly meet "the other" in as many ways as possible, reported problems while completing assignments together. Difficulties were often related to language issues and communication styles, and sometimes just to differences in personality.

If postgraduate students who choose to study a degree in International Communication encounter these problems, what does this mean for diverse student groups in other subjects? If it is so difficult to access intercultural communication in a class where awareness and knowledge of theories is a given, where everyone brings in some previous experience and skills in intercultural communication, how can universities equip all students, regardless of their field of study, with the intercultural skills graduates need and are expected to have in a rapidly globalizing world? Where does "emotional intelligence" and "cultural intelligence" come from? What do students need to be prepared for the global knowledge society, and what does it mean to be transcultural? Key terms such as globalization, cultural hybridity, hybrid identity, intercultural, transcultural and cross-cultural are being used in various contexts and at times become so vague and void that it is hard to attach any meaning to them.

I was looking for material for a lecture about the concept of intercultural competence in education when I stumbled across American, European and Australian university websites announcing that their graduates would leave the university as interculturally competent and well rounded personalities. The school of civil engineering and architecture in Kärnten, Austria, to name only one, states that

> In an increasingly globalised world, intercultural competence is a key professional qualification in every field. This demands both a reflective view on the growing multicultural diversity in one's homeland as well as looking out beyond one's own borders (http://www.fh-kaernten.at/en/civil-engineering-and-architecture/bachelor/civil-engineering.html).

Finding closer definitions of what that actually means was difficult and the results were scarce, though I found scattered examples of university policies, course offerings, academic support and intercultural programs that reflect an awareness of the need of intercultural dialogue in theory and practice. Using Macquarie University as an example, I aimed at defining intercultural competence as a graduate capability for university students and at finding out if related skills could and should be assessed.

When I decided on an approach to define intercultural competence at universities, I contacted Dr Darla Deardorff who had used the Delphi method to investigate intercultural competence in the US. It was her spontaneous support and encouragement that made me go ahead with this project. She and Prof Dr Hartmut Schröder whose work on intercultural communication and taboo has influenced me for years, gave continuous support and advice related to each stage of this study. It was a pleasure to have them on board and their opinions and suggestions throughout the process helped shape the results.

I am especially grateful to Ms Kristina Wolters, who successfully completed her MA in International Communication at Macquarie University, for her practical participation in this research project. In particular, her involvement in all phases of the student survey and her work with the student focus group was invaluable for this project. It was great to have a companion who contributes fresh ideas, attention to detail and a good sense of humour to the task.

I am deeply indebted to all student participants who filled in questionnaires and especially to the six students who also engaged in the focus group during a busy time when major papers and exams were due. Their input on the outcome of this study is indelible.

A Delphi Study depends on the continuous support of its participants, and it can easily fall to nothing if some of them decide to drop out – which they could, at any stage. I therefore thank my 21 colleagues who dedicated their time and lent their expertise to this study, for making themselves available over a longer period of time, for their patience with extended questionnaires, for their emails, comments and encouragement. I wish to extend my thanks to all colleagues who supported the project by advertising it to their students or by allowing Kristina and me to visit their classrooms. The person who helped make this project readable is my colleague Dr Joanna Penglase, I thank her for polishing and re-organising mobile pieces of text.

A big thank you goes to the team at Cambridge Scholars, especially to Amanda Millar and Soucin Yip-Sou for all their patient help in putting this book together.

Last but not least I thank Macquarie University for financing this study through a Macquarie Social Inclusion Grant.

FOREWORD

The term *Intercultural Competence* has become a key issue in many countries, both within the framework of political discussions and academic discourses. However, the circumstances vary from one country to another, which becomes especially apparent in the comparison between Australia and Germany. Germany shares borders with several other countries, and therefore the meaning of *Intercultural Competence* is different from the meaning of the term in Australia. In Germany the term is always related to intercultural encounters in relation to crossing borders. This leads automatically to dialogues with neighbours, which may depict more an effort to make sense of the other than meaningful dialogue, understanding and effective and successful communication. This seems to remain untouched by political action within the framework of the European Union (EU) which aims to demonstrate that borders have become so-called "permeable borders". In contrast, Australia can be seen as a country without shared borders and direct neighbours. This, however, does not change the important point that this country with its various waves of migration has always been a multicultural society and increasingly an example of successful globalization since the abolition of the white Australia policy in the 1970s.

In Germany, *Intercultural Competence* did not come into being as a concept that created public and academic interest until the 1980s, a point in time when it had finally become clear that Germany, too, had developed as a country of migration and globalization, which has had a deep impact on all areas of public and private life. Australia however, from the time it was colonized, has consisted of various emigrant groups who bring together all their cultural embossing and so contribute to a further, multicultural development of the state. How do these groups relate to each other? How do they act towards those who originally "owned" the country?

Another difference between Germany and Australia lays in the fact that Australia is not perceived as a typical „modern nation" of industry that exports manufactured goods, but it is more similar to countries which had previously been seen as inferior due to unconventional and relatively unknown economic behaviour. Thus in Australia agricultural products, coal and metals are important export products.

Furthermore, because of its size and its history that is intertwined with that of Europe, Australia has alienated itself from its geopolitical past. For this reason *Intercultural Competence* as a socio-cultural phenomenon shows its effects, for instance, in the realms of religion and economy, but also in its deep impact on the relationship between different generations (within the country) and their handling of the old and new "cultural heritage". In Australia, the discourse on the meaning of *Intercultural Competence* mainly occurs within the country, not outside of it. So, Sabine Krajewski and colleagues at Macquarie University set out to explore what the term *Intercultural Competence* actually means in an Australian context. European observers, for example, may be asking themselves whether multiculturalism in Australia is a basic truth of everyday life, or whether there is no functional multicultural society but rather a multisectorial one down under.

While intercultural situations in Australia mainly arise within the various groups of immigrants, we can assume that intercultural encounters in Europe are not only related to multiculturalism, but also to contact situations in border regions. This means that such situations are always related to complex, historical contexts. This important difference possibly also explains why the academic discourses around intercultural competence in Germany are much more theoretical, in part explicitly philosophically oriented and "intercultural trainings" achieve higher value than elsewhere. Especially now, with the shift from industrial to service society and at the end of the era of European and North American dominance over the world, it is essential to combine theory and practice of intercultural competence in the universities. In current times, at European universities it is still the case that the term *Intercultural Competence* is discussed in a theoretical way and that its practical use in economic life is more or less successful.

In Australia however, for a long time it seemed that the discussion of *Intercultural Competence* was superfluous: A strong migration and its positive effects on the economy and everyday life were regarded as a matter of course, so that research and academic study of intercultural communication at universities in general were seen more as a luxury than a necessity. Everyday life itself solved possible problems (more or less successfully, at times on behalf of the established and to the disadvantage of the weak). Despite many differences between Australia and Germany, herein lies a common ground of both countries: In both it is obvious that intercultural contact alone does not automatically lead to understanding and to *Intercultural Competence*, and it also does not lead to a development of a common identity. Sometimes it leads more to misunderstanding and provokes conflict situations rather than coming to understanding and successful communication. This can be demonstrated by using the instance of cities in (German/Polish) border regions such as Frankfurt (Oder)/Słubice. Successful communication does not only depend on being able to use a certain level of the relevant foreign language, but it depends mainly on the overall context. In his book "Kulturschock Deutschland" (culture shock Germany), Wolf Wagner discusses the phenomenon of "culture shock" and shows current difficulties in German/German contact situations (here, the situation and relationship in question is between Germans of the former east side/GDR and Germans of the former west side/FRG). Wagner assumes that communication leads to understanding if the following criteria are met:

- both groups have the same (social) position or the representative of the minority has a higher (social) level,
- the authority supports the contact,
- the encounters take place regularly and each involved party has a close relationship to each other,
- the contact is related to important conventions of behaviour and key experiences,
- both parties in the encounters benefit from it,
- the contact is pleasant and promotes further contact,
- there are common goals (which help to overcome differences),
- aims of the contact and their results are emphasized (and goals which stress differences are less important),
- a positive, social climate.

However, an escalation of problems is possible if the following occur:

- the situation produces competition,
- if one party of the involved groups is losing face or prestige,
- if someone feels frustration and disappointment,
- if the cultural and moral expectations for all involved parties are not acceptable,
- if the representative of the minority has a lower social status.

In addition, Krajewski's research confirms that *(...) even in a place where positive circumstances pave the way to successful intercultural communication, namely in intercultural and multilingual classrooms, guided intervention is crucial to achieving intercultural competence.*

For this reason we should ruminate over whether the concept of *Intercultural Competence* is enough to discuss all phenomena connected with it. The problem lays in the fact that (in Europe) only part of society, the highly educated part, deals with *Intercultural Competence* and its difficulties. But even within the context of this highly educated society, people use their *Intercultural Competence* only in a very superficial way: *Intercultural Competence* is only seen here as an ability to understand each other, but to understand each other is not enough to avoid conflicts or to deal with deeper cultural differences that can, in the worst case, even lead to military actions. Real communication and understanding takes place only if people gain competences in how to deal with conflicts and learn strategies which are summarized as a "competence in cultural mediation". Such knowledge and herewith connected competence is especially necessary for people who live in border areas. Ideally, a competent "cultural mediator" would be able to recognize key issues which could lead to conflicts and could help to avoid them. Furthermore, mediators could be useful in highlighting reasons for difficulties and misunderstandings and could demonstrate possible communication strategies which lead to relaxed and successful communication. Skilled cultural mediators in general would be very important in the area of education and in mass media.

Finally, we should pose the question, whether the term "intercultural" should be better replaced by another term. According to the opinion of Hildebrand (2006), intercultural behaviour aims to overcome cultural conflict by holding intercultural dialogue, but at the same time it operates with a traditional term referring to homogenous cultures aspiring to separation (this depicts the scientific position of the Herder tradition). If we insist on a traditional term, we support a non-exchange between cultures when difficulties arise with representatives of different cultures who are unable to find common ground for communication.

Sabine Krajewski comes to a similar conclusion, having analyzed the concept of *Intercultural Competence* and establishing that most models of *Intercultural Competence* present positions only from a western point of view. The co-existence of culture-specific models may strengthen differences between cultures and contribute to communication that may be counterproductive to building meaningful relationships. The concept of transculturalism, developed in the 1990s (see Welsch, 1995), consists of the primary assumption that cultures are characterized by a plurality of different identities and permeable borders. A typical indicator of such cultures are interlinked communication structures as a consequence of migration, and further developing material and immaterial networks (e.g.

internet, international traffic) in conjunction with economic interdependencies. Welsch (1995) proposes the point of view that in the framework of a cultural formation, the importance of national cultures and single languages is reduced, replaced by a global culture developed with a large range of interdependencies. In the sense of intercultural contact situations, this means that transcultural networks depict encounters which are orientated towards common grounds, while—at the same time— consisting of differences. Transculturalism produces diversity not only within a culture, but also in an external way. This means that individuals are ramblers between cultures, swaying between identities; they have to accept new norms and attitudes, while simultaneously passing on their own norms and attitudes. People here have to learn how to handle discontinuity in the most appropriate way. In such processes, cultural borders are regularly negotiated. Regional identities no longer exist (Hildebrand 2006).

With gratitude it is my aim now to remember that thanks to Sabine Krajewski's critical appraisal of the topic, questions of multiculturalism, interculturalism and transculturalism move into the background.

The aim of her project is explicated in the Macquarie model of intercultural competence. European models are dominated by diagrams in which arrows originate somewhere and end elsewhere to show how elements of intercultural competence relate to each other. Sabine Krajewski lets the elements generated through her study interlock in a circular frame; they are interdependent and keep "the machine" going. This practical approach leaves room for development and change: the machine is build by many; toothed wheels may be added on or moved in opposite directions. Intercultural competence therefore does not rely on the machine itself but on the people designing it. This is our space for further discussion and development within our intercultural world.

Hartmut Schröder

Literature

Hildebrand, Mark (2006): *Inter- vs. Transkulturalität. Die deutsche Sprach im deutsch-deutschen Austausch nach der Wiedervereinigung.* In: *Zeitschrift für Angewandte Linguistik,* Peter Lang GmbH: Frankfurt/Main, p. 122 f.

Wagner, Wolf (1996), Kulturschock Deutschland. Hamburg: Rotbuch.

Welsch, Wolfgang (1995), Transkulturalität. In: Institut für Auslandsbeziehungen (Ed.): Migration und Kultureller Wandel, Schwerpunktthema der Zeitschrift für Kulturaustausch, 45(1), Stuttgart.

CHAPTER ONE

INTERNATIONALIZATION AND INTERCULTURAL COMPETENCE

I know that you believe you understand what you think I said, but I'm not sure you realize that what you heard is not what I meant.
—Robert McCloskey (1914-2003)

INTRODUCTION

DARLA K. DEARDORFF

An engineer works on a virtual team with colleagues on 4 different continents. A newly minted school teacher who has never been outside her own country faces a classroom with students from 15 different countries. A business woman whose parents are from 2 different countries, grew up in 3 cultures, speaks 4 languages fluently, attended a university in another country and now works in a country she has only visited previously as a tourist. These scenarios are realities in the 21st century.

Consider this: We are currently preparing students for jobs and technologies that don't yet exist ... in order to solve problems we don't even know are problems yet. And even currently known global problems are seemingly insurmountable, some of which are outlined in the United Nations Millenium Development Goals which include ending poverty and hunger, universal education, gender equality, combating HIV/AIDs, and achieving environmental sustainability. Albert Einstein once said, "We can't solve problems by using the same kind of thinking we used when we created them." So, what do students need to know and do in the 21st century to tackle these global problems? One response is that students need "21st century skills" which are often referred to broadly as "intercultural" or "global" competence. Indeed, one study concluded that "the intensity of globalisation (sic) in recent years has brought intercultural competence acquisition studies back to the center (sic) stage" (Kuada, 2004, p. 10). Thus, intercultural competence development is and will play an ever greater role in the future given the growing diversity of society and within the workplace.

Yet, what is intercultural competence? Intercultural competence is an oft-discussed but rarely understood and defined term within the field of international education and beyond. This term is currently a "hot topic" within higher education in the United States as well as in other countries, with questions being asked about how post-secondary institutions can help students develop intercultural competence. Given this growing importance of intercultural competence within post-secondary education, it becomes imperative to more closely examine what this concept is and how best to develop and assess it in our students. If educators are to be successful in helping students become more interculturally competent, it is important to explore definitions and frameworks of intercultural competence, some of which have been debated and discussed for several decades, much of it within the United States and Europe (see Spitzberg and Changnon, 2009).

Based on my work on intercultural competence, which provided the first grounded-research based framework on this concept in the U.S., leading experts in the United States agreed on one essential element of intercultural competence, that of understanding the world from others' perspectives (Deardorff, 2006). Thus, it becomes imperative to explore different cultural perspectives on what it means to be successful in interacting with those from different backgrounds. In reviewing literature from other countries and regions of the world on various cultural perspectives on intercultural competence (Bordas, 2007; Chen & An, 1009; Kim, 2002; Imahori & Lanigan, 1989; Manian & Naidu, 2009; Medina & Siningen, 2009; Mato, 2009; Miike, 2003; Moosmueller & Schoenhuth, 2009; Nwosu, 2009; Nydell, 2005; Taylor & Nwosu, 2001; Ting-Toomey, 2009; Zaharna, 2009; see also a report written for UNESCO, *A comparative analysis and global perspective of regional studies on intercultural competence* by Deardorff, 2010), several overarching themes emerge. Those include the importance of relationship in intercultural competence, the necessity of considering historical, social and economic contexts (especially in immigrant societies and those with a history of colonialism), the crucial role that identity plays in intercultural competence, and the need for cultural humility, which consists of both a strong sense of cultural self-awareness and recognition of multiple viewpoints coupled with respect -of truly valuing others from diverse backgrounds.

This study by Sabine Krajewski at Macquarie University adds yet another valuable contribution to understanding intercultural competence as it explores a definition of intercultural competence from an Australian perspective, using a Delphi methodology within the context of Macquarie University. This study explores the opinions of both students and staff at Macquarie University regarding the identification of intercultural skills and relevant learning and teaching leading to the development of intercultural competence in students. The resulting intercultural competence model and related project outcomes may be used by Macquarie and other institutions seeking to apply and integrate intercultural competence into the curriculum. Ultimately, these frameworks and definitions from the various studies that have been conducted to date on intercultural competence, including this Macquarie study, can be used to guide higher education efforts in helping students not only get along better with those from different cultures, but to work together to address pressing global challenges that confront humankind in the 21st century.

CULTURE, COMMUNICATION AND IDENTITY

Any work on intercultural competence needs to include reflections on central concepts such as culture, communication, and identity.

In Bordieu's (1973) framework of social power, culture is a form of capital. People who have access to a general set of dominant cultural values and norms will have an advantage over those who were socialised in a different culture and have different sets of cultural capital at their disposal. Power relations are influenced by the different cultural dispositions. This becomes visible in plural societies where different ethnic groups co-exist in one social space, each following their own rules and regulations. As soon as they interact in the public sphere of the market place, the moral control that regulates behaviour within each group falls apart so that one group can simply oppress another. (Rex in Guibernau and Rex, p. 219) Such plural societies are inherently unequal and counterproductive to social cohesion because they focus on the individual and on individual ethnic groups rather than on the overall community.

The notion that 'culture is ordinary' (Williams, 1958) and describes a whole way of life rather than ethnic background and values alone, has become widely accepted. Hansen and Lynch, (2005, p. 23), expand that notion when they stress that values and beliefs are being shaped not by culture, language, ethnicity and race alone, but by numerous other factors such as socioeconomic status, educational level, and personal experience. Categorizing people as similar because of their linguistic and cultural backgrounds means to merely stereotype. It is important to keep in mind that culture is only one of many features that defines individuals and it may not always be the most important one, yet culture is inseparable from the concept of identity, and it is a part that is not static but constantly changing.

Discussing intercultural competence means discussing communication. After all, one of the main goals of intercultural competence training is successful communication with people from various cultural backgrounds. All interpersonal communication is laden with physical, semantic, or psychological noise which can be seen as unwanted signals that disrupt the communication process and affect the meaning to be shared (see basic communication models such as Shannon and Weaver, 1949). Communication across cultures and peoples may be even more prone to misunderstanding and conflict, so it makes sense to be prepared for conflict and to develop some skills to "repair" communication gone wrong (Ting–Toomey, 1997). In intercultural communication theory (Gudykunst and Ting-Toomey, 1988; Gudykunst and Kim, 1992), culture and communication are inseparable; they depend on and constitute each other. The way people communicate is influenced by their culture. Most Asian cultures, for example, are high context cultures: they rely more on the context in which communication occurs than on the verbal message itself. Western cultures such as the US or European cultures rely mainly on verbal communication, they are low context cultures. The dimension of high and low context is part of Hofstede's framework of categorizing national cultures from the 1980s, but it has been an integral part of later intercultural communication theory such as Ting-Toomey's work on conflict management (1993) or Gudykunst's theory of anxiety and uncertainty management (1988, 1993). More recent research (Parker et al., 2009) indicates that the divide between high and low context cultures may be closing because of globalization and the resulting increased interaction and communication between people, particularly as a result of increasing education and business connections. This would mean that globalization leads to mixed identities and communication styles. However, as Paquet (2008) points out in his book about deep cultural diversity, the "legitimization of 'hybrid identities' based on a plurality of participations in ethnie, nation, and civil society, has not developed evenly across national territories."

Though the term *hybridity* literally means mixture, it has been discussed (and rejected) in numerous discourses about its meaning and connotations (it has, for example, along with globalization been rejected for allowing and even inviting cultural imperialism (Turnstall, 1977; Castells, 1997; Baumann, 1997). Bhaba (1994), on the other hand, takes a postcolonial approach and interprets the term not only as a mixture of two or more cultural backgrounds, but as a combination that produces a *third space* in which new identities can be produced. This new space offers new possibilities of cultural interpretations and is therefore a production site for new cultural meanings. In Kraidy's view (2005), hybridity goes beyond coexistence and sharing values in the public sphere, it is a new creation, a result of parting and re-arranging cultural identities. He assumes that, since every culture has traces of other cultures and is to some extent mixed already, increasing hybridity is the cultural logic of globalization (Kraidy, 2005, p. 148). Globalization is not something we can prevent from happening as the resistance expressed in *glocalization* is part of globalization itself, and consequently separate cultures are a thing of the past. Diversity is a result of globalization and it is neither something to wish for nor something to be afraid of, it is a fact of life.

GLOBALIZATION AND HYBRID IDENTITIES: AUSTRALIA'S *LIVING IN HARMONY* CONCEPT

Since the 1970s, Australia describes itself as a multicultural country and keeps interpreting and re-evaluating the idea of multiculturalism. Multicultural societies can be, but are not per se, compatible with the idea of equality. There are two important days in Australia that reflect the country's official attitude towards itself as an immigration country and towards diversity issues in particular. *Australia Day* is a public holiday, celebrated on January 26 each year. It marks the arrival of the First Fleet at Botany Bay, which makes it a somewhat controversial celebration because it also marks the beginning of injustice towards the aboriginal people in Australia. Today, Australia Day tends to be a family-oriented event accompanied by festive speeches and culminating in fireworks. Australia pays tribute to its indigenous communities and voices its commitment to new citizens, for some of whom it is a special privilege to become an Australian citizen on that symbolic day.

Australia has learnt from its history and come a long way since the abolition of the White Australia policy in the 1970s. In February 2008, the then Prime Minister's (Kevin Rudd) official apology to the indigenous people of Australia on behalf of the Australian government set a milestone in finally implementing the respect and equality that the country identified as of highest value in living diversity.

The other important day, though it is not a public holiday like *Australia Day*, is *Harmony Day* which is celebrated on 21 March every year. Harmony day is an initiative to create awareness and to celebrate diversity in schools and local communities and the activities are supported by the government, communities and local businesses. It is part of the *Living in Harmony Program* which was introduced by the government in 1998 to promote mutual respect, Australian values, community participation and a sense of belonging for everyone (Wood and Landry, 2007, p. 275). The *Living in Harmony* program was established and administered by the former Department of Immigration and Multicultural Affairs (DIMA) which is now the Department of Immigration and Citizenship (DIAC). In their article on the Australian model of multiculturalism, Syed and Kramar (2010, p. 99) point out that the removal of the word *multicultural* from the name of the department in 2007 suggests that multiculturalism is no longer a priority at government policy level. However, under the new government in 2009, the name of the *Living in Harmony* initiative was changed to *Diverse Australia Program (diversity and social cohesion program)*, promoting that 'everyone belongs'.

It is interesting to take a moment and think about what exactly Australian values are and what images people in other countries have of the Australian way of life. The *Living in Harmony* Program lists *respect, fairness* and *equality for all* as distinct Australian values. This sounds progressive and reflects Australia as well prepared for globalization processes, but what does *equality for all*, for example, really mean in everyday life and on a community level? If it means equal rights before the law, does it also mean equal participation in decision processes? Australia sees itself as a multicultural society where a diversity of cultural values and individual beliefs co-exist under the umbrella of the overall Australian culture and its distinct national values (note the difference to plural societies where this "umbrella of overall culture" does not exist). This is reminiscent of studies that divide the public and the private sphere and then show how they overlap and interfere with each other, in terms of education for example. The realm of customs and beliefs regarding relationships and marriage may be clearly matters belonging to the private sphere, but these matters will be discussed and influenced by schools and universities, though education as an institutionalized entity belongs to the public sphere. This is where the Australian model would profit from the idea of a *third space* in the sense Bhaba uses it. What exactly this means needs to be looked at in light of the definition of multicultural societies. In fact, Germany's chancellor Angela Merkel recently claimed that the attempt at multiculturalism in her country had failed (BBC News 17/10/10. http://www.bbc.co.uk/news/world-europe-11559451).

Germany is a comparatively small country that invited guest workers in the post war economic boom times of the 1960s and 70s, attempting to become a guest-working country rather than a culturally diverse society, which is completely different from Australian immigration patterns in the past. Full community integration and a shared identity were simply not an option for the immigrants to Germany of fifty years ago, and many of them had never planned on staying in Germany either.

Chris Bowen (Minister for Immigration and Citizenship) recently introduced Australia's new multiculturalism strategy, claiming that for a government to be free and equal, it has to be multicultural, and vice versa.

The government will introduce a new independent advisory body, the Australian multicultural council, with broader terms of reference, to succeed the current advisory council. The new body will act as a champion for multiculturalism in the community, will advise government on multicultural affairs, and will help ensure Australian government services will respond to the needs of migrant and refugee communities. We will also establish a national anti-racism partnership and strategy to design and deliver that anti-racism strategy (Bowen, 16 Feb 2011, in his podcast on multiculturalism in the Australian context).

Neither the German nor the Australian approach focuses on the creation of new identities and each version distinguishes between private and public spheres. In his article about multicultural and plural societies, Rex (2005) points out that sharing core values may still leave space for the individual to be free to also live and express norms and values attached to other cultural spaces, but this is problematic because of the ways in which public and private spheres interfere with each other.

Australia still has work to do to become an inclusive society, but as Dunn et al. (2007) show in their long-term study about racism in Australia, other places such as Europe or the US certainly are not any further along in building successful multicultural societies. One of the reasons for this may be the fact that Germany and France have not invited immigrants to fully participate in the public sphere, another may be that the concept of multiculturalism does not work well in its present versions and negative effects such as inequality and racism prevail.

A key finding from the racism project is that while racism is quite prevalent in Australian society, its occurrences differ from place to place. These variations have been largely overlooked by anti-racism campaigns in Australia. The findings show that most Australians recognise that racism is a problem in society. Racist attitudes are positively associated with age, non-tertiary education, and to a slightly lesser extent with those who do not speak a language other than English, the Australia-born, and with males (http://www.uws.edu.au/arts/coa/professorial_lecture_series/prof_kevin_dunn).

The Australian Minister for Immigration and Citizenship acknowledges that Australian diversity has been of incredible advantage to the country in terms of economic as well as cultural benefits and the innovative forces that come with it. He claims that each generation has expressed some anxiety about new migration groups, implying that it takes some time to get used to each other but that in the end migrants come "not to change our values but because of them" (Bowen, 16 Feb 2011, in his podcast on multiculturalism in the Australian context). This may or may not be the case, but no matter whether migrants intend to change dominant values or not, successful migration includes passing on and sharing values, both of the dominant and of minority cultures. Multicultural societies are not about the dominant culture and new migration groups 'getting used to each other', but about negotiating new identities.

It is of vital importance for the development of *Diverse Australia* to keep communicating about diversity issues. *Living in Harmony* may well be an inscription above the entrance door of a retirement village, it shares the pacifying qualities of common terminology such as "social inclusion", "social cohesion" and "cultural awareness" that is being used by politicians and educators without ensuring consensus about what they mean. The difference between 'Living in Harmony' and 'Diverse Australia' lies in the concepts behind these terms and the subtle differences that can be read as multiculturalism vs. shared identity, separate cultures striving for the same rights vs. people sharing a third space and sharing responsibilities. One of the connotations of multicultural societies is that they may represent a federation of various cultures who share a space (like plural societies), while diversity refers to a group of people from different cultures who create and share core values.

Appreciating diversity does not happen overnight and "communicating across cultures and peoples does not come naturally" (Wood and Landry, 2008, p.5). To be equal does not mean to be the same, and unfortunately those who are different do suffer discrimination. Communities and nation states do need to face up to the issues related to diversity and implement strategies to encourage different perspectives and to mediate diversity.

INTERNATIONALIZATION AND INTERCULTURAL COMPETENCE AT UNIVERSITIES

In universities across the world, 'intercultural communication' is being offered as a teaching unit in disciplines such as international business, anthropology, media and communications, modern languages, and others. It is an interdisciplinary field and at some European and US American universities, Master degrees in intercultural communication are already being offered, though it is not yet fully recognised as a discipline in its own right (Prechtl and Lund, 2007). Intercultural communication sets out to connect universality and diversity. It involves communicative competences that enable people from different backgrounds to successfully relate to each other. As Lynch and Hanson (2005, p. 67) point out in their work about developing cross-cultural competence, people [in the United States] speak openly and publicly about almost everything, including topics around sexuality, personal hygiene and other issues that used to be 'hidden' and taboo. They claim, however, that 'discussions of cultural, racial, ethnic and language diversity between members of different groups are rarely heard' (p. 67) and imply that differences in skin colour are visible but verbally taboo. Surely in universities this will not apply, as university discourse lends itself to temporary 'taboo lifting' (Schroeder & Krajewski, 2009)? The academic environment should be an ideal context in which to explore similarities and differences openly and respectfully and thereby create interactions that dispel myths and open doors to understanding, but is this a matter of course?

The terms 'intercultural competence' and 'intercultural communicative competence' are often used interchangeably, though intercultural communicative competence focuses on the communicative element and linguistic awareness to a greater degree. In this project, both terms will be used.

There is no fixed definition of intercultural competence, it continues to evolve. With increasing (student) mobility since the middle of the 20th century, groundbreaking work on intercultural and cross-cultural experience has emerged, including various definitions of culture shock (Oberg 1960,

Adler 1974, Paige 1990, Anderson 1994); communicative competence (Hymes 1971); work in foreign language teaching and intercultural competence (Kramsch 1993, Byram 1997). Intercultural skills and the competence to communicate effectively and appropriately in cross-cultural settings are indispensable, especially for young graduates who set out looking to develop international careers. The need to make intercultural competence part of the internationalization process of higher education and to offer a learning environment that develops relevant skills as graduate capabilities has been recognised, but there is a gap between that recognition and implementing a clear strategy towards achieving that goal. (See also McAllister et al. 2006). Most university websites claim that their students will gain intercultural competence while completing their degrees, but the term is neither defined nor does it seem to be measurable. Assuming that intercultural competence is a skill, it should be possible to assess it and to document its existence and progress. If intercultural competence is an ongoing process, measurement can only reflect a moment in time; it can reflect the ability to communicate effectively in a particular circumstance and situation only.

Intercultural competence first needs to be defined and its different aspects and stages made explicit to create awareness and aims for development. It may then be possible to assess intercultural competence by using a mix of quantitative and qualitative methods which may include self – and peer – observation, interviews and case studies.

Intercultural Competence as Part of Quality Teaching and a Graduate Capability of Macquarie Students

This project aims at finding a definition for intercultural competence based on consensus between academic staff and students at Macquarie University (also referred to as MQ). Using this definition and existing models of intercultural competence, a dynamic, flexible MQ model will emerge which can be used as a basis to develop training sessions for teaching and learning intercultural skills.

Macquarie University has a dynamic mix of staff from all over the world, many of whom have expertise in intercultural communication and intercultural competence issues. This project will bring some of these experts and their experience together and find out if they can agree on the nature of intercultural competence and how it can best be measured. The Delphi method, first used in the 1950s to forecast the effects of military strategies, is a mean of getting experts together without the constraints of time and space. The researcher moderates a communication process in which each participant gives their opinion on a specific question and in the further process reflects on the opinions expressed by themselves and others. This research tool permits researchers to combine the reports or testimony of a group of experts into one, useful statement. (Stitt-Gohdes & Crews 2004). This project employs the Delphi method to form consensus and to prepare a definition of intercultural competence.

Students are a vital part of the university and their voice needs to be heard in all aspects of university life. The University of Turku, for example, describes their students as active participants in the development of education:

> The students of the University are members of the university community who, in addition to teachers, have a central role in the development of education. University studies are basically an interaction between the parties involved, and students contribute to the teaching situations with their own input. Regarding students as patrons of education, who are offered educational services according to their preferences, would be to

undervalue their position as university community members. (http://www.utu.fi/en/university/quality/students.html)

Therefore, the current study also includes the opinions of two hundred students from across all faculties at Macquarie University because it aims to compare and, if possible, combine opinions about intercultural competence of staff and students at MQ. The student questionnaire does not provide feedback like the Delphi study but consists of answer suggestions common in intercultural competence literature for students to rank and add to. Where compatible, the outcome will be compared to items created during the Delphi process. A student focus group session will be used to discuss results of the student survey in more detail.

Macquarie will be the first Australian university that has a definition of intercultural competence based on consensus of students and staff. Our model of intercultural competence will be based on existing models that are being used elsewhere (e.g. Byram's model of intercultural communicative competence in Europe, Deardorff's Pyramid model and Process model in the US) but have a distinct MQ touch. All parts of the project involve the use of existent expertise in the field of intercultural communication and intercultural competence at Macquarie University as well as the recommendations and evaluations of two experts from outside institutions; Prof. Schröder is chair of Social Linguistics and Media and Head of the Institute for Trans-Cultural Health Studies at the European University Viadrina, Frankfurt (Oder), Germany. Dr. Deardorff is Executive Director of the Association of International Education Administrators, a national professional organization headquartered at Duke University, North Carolina, USA. She teaches cross-cultural courses at Duke University and served as a consultant on assessment and intercultural competence development to universities and non-profit organizations in different countries.

The present study is modelled on the Deardorff study (2004), which resulted in the first grounded research based definition of ICC from a US perspective, in using the Delphi technique to achieve consensus about the concept of intercultural competence and to explore if intercultural competence can and should be measured. While the experts contributing to Deardorff's study are leading intercultural scholars from across the US (plus 1 participant from the UK and 1 from Canada), the present study is based on an expert panel selected among teaching staff in one Australian University.

The initial questions of Delphi round 1 are those used by Deardorff and they have the same limitations: The first question 'what constitutes intercultural competence' presupposes that we agree on definitions of the terms 'culture', 'intercultural' and 'competence'. The second question, 'how can intercultural competence best be measured', implies that it can be measured. The current study refers to IC (intercultural competence) but picks up the term ICC (intercultural communicative competence) when this term is referred to by members of the expert panel.

There are many attempts to conclusively define the term culture and various models to visualise the abstract term (such as the Iceberg model by Selfridge and Sokolik (1975), E.T. Hall (1976), W. L. French and C. H. Bell in 1979 or the Onion model (Hofstede 1991). As with all abstract terms there is no clear common understanding of culture, but in this context it will be useful to adapt existing models and think of cultural practice, language, norms, beliefs and values that shape culture.

Intercultural competence is always part of a lifelong learning process that very much depends on personal attitudes and openness. There is a variety of skills that can be taught and learned as well as measured, but if intercultural competence as an overall ability can be measured is questionable. As Deardorff (2009) points out in her work, it is important to concentrate on a few aspects of intercultural competence at a time, use multiple qualitative and quantitative tools and not depend on one person alone to assess another person's intercultural skills. In the process of this project, these skills and relevant learning and teaching methods will be identified.

There are plenty of reasons why intercultural competence should become a graduate capability of university students: Employers are looking for well-rounded graduates who have the flexibility and cultural intelligence needed in a rapidly globalising world. Therefore, intercultural communication skills will facilitate access to and participation in the work force. Graduate capabilities add characteristics to all students, regardless of their field of study. Ideally they emerge from their universities as lifelong learners who are active and engaged citizens wherever they go.

Once a university has decided which capabilities are valuable for their students, it will explore how it can assess if students have those capabilities when they graduate. It seems to be difficult to test generic skills, but there is a demand to develop teaching and learning strategies that demonstrate achievement and progress without relying on traditional exams. Developing graduate capabilities such as intercultural competence is a *formative* learning process and it may be possible to measure selected skills in a specific circumstance but not the capability as a whole. The introduction of participation units (involvement in practical community projects) at Macquarie is an example of acknowledging the importance of experiences that will enhance the overall learning of university students and create transferable 'life skills'. A "graduate capabilities framework" such as the one developed by MQ scholars depicted below, suggests means and expressions of personal attributes and general skills that students are expected to gain during their studies. This is, of course, a model and students will bring to class, develop and achieve these skills to varying degrees.

The intercultural competence model and other project outcomes of this project may be used by MQ and other institutions seeking to apply a model of intercultural competence and to integrate intercultural competence into the university curriculum as a graduate capability.

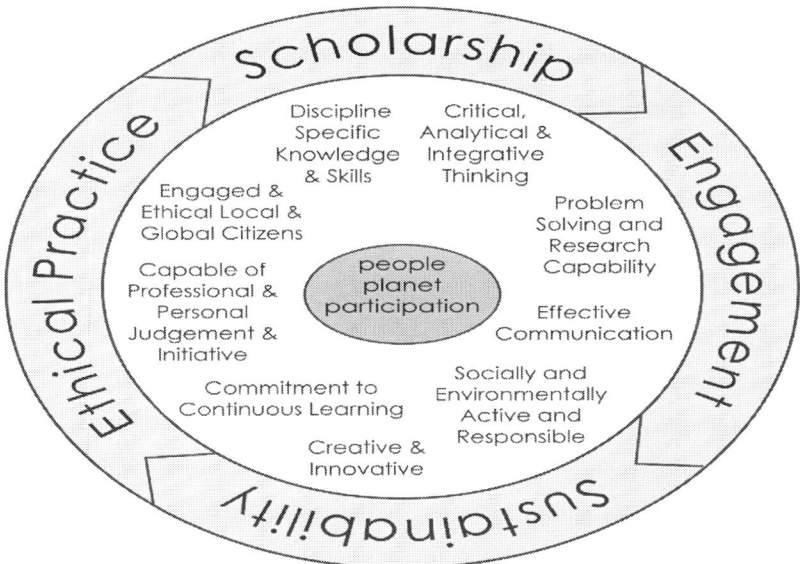

Fig. 1-1: MQ Graduate Capabilities Framework:
http://www.mq.edu.au/ltc/projects/curriculum_renewal/graduate_capabilities.htm

INTERNATIONALIZATION: A BRIEF SURVEY IN PREPARATION OF THE STUDY

To generate names for the expert panel, a preliminary survey was sent via email to deans and associate deans of the 4 faculties, to Macquarie International and to the Institute of Social Inclusion. Participants were asked to name up to 5 people within Macquarie University who have expertise in intercultural communication and/or intercultural competence and might be candidates to participate in this study as part of an expert panel. Relevant publications, teaching or other work experience in the field, relevant experience abroad, membership in certain committees or other aspects were listed as indicators of intercultural expertise. The response rate was average for a questionnaire distributed via email (13 respondents out of 48). See Appendix 1 for results of this survey, and the 6 questions it asked.

CHAPTER TWO:

A DELPHI STUDY ABOUT INTERCULTURAL COMPETENCE AT MACQUARIE UNIVERSITY

There never were in the world two opinions alike, no more than two hairs
or two grains; the most universal quality is diversity.
—Michel de Montaigne

THE DELPHI METHOD

As noted above, the Delphi Method is a technique where a researcher generates information by asking a selected panel of people with expertise in a certain matter about their opinion on that subject. It usually focuses on a complex problem or task which is to be discussed via a series of questionnaires sent via email.

In the beginning, individual responses are being collected, in subsequent rounds the experts are being asked to rank or comment on all comments made by the group. Advantages of the method are that the group of experts does not have to meet but may be geographically disperse and complete each round in their own time. It also ensures anonymity among participants which allows free expression without human interference that might take place in a face to face interaction of the group, such as the influence of any dominant group members.

The method is partly qualitative (particularly in the first round where answers need to be itemized and fed back to the panel for evaluation) and partly quantitative (in subsequent rounds, means and standard deviation decide on which item is to be further discussed and which is not). The researcher moderates the group by using Delphi as a communication structure through which the collective opinion of the expert group can be surveyed (Helmer, 1983). Controlled feedback allows each of the panellists to re-examine and independently judge items as presented and shared by all group members, which includes revising their own initial ideas. After each round the results are analysed and communicated back to the participants. Ideally the group exercise will progress until consensus has been achieved. Statistical group response ensures that each member's opinion is represented in the final response (Dalkey et al., 1972). The research instruments (questionnaires 1, 2 and 3) were given to other researchers (Schröder and Deardorff, see p. 15) to establish face validity. Their comments were used to improve questions, format and scales.

THE DELPHI STUDY:
PRE-SURVEY

Thirty names were suggested by participants of the internationalization round. Additional prospective participants were chosen from the university websites using relevant research records or an expression of special interest in intercultural communication or intercultural competence as selection criteria. A further 11 were selected in this way. A preliminary questionnaire was sent to possible participants of the expert panel. This survey had several functions:

- ask possible participants to self-evaluate if they are experts in the field of intercultural communication and/or intercultural competence
- ask some general questions that would not fit the Delphi format but will provide background information
- invite people to the Delphi study and ask for their ongoing support during the project

The pre-Delphi questionnaire and an information and consent form that was approved by the university's ethics committee was sent out via email. Of the forty-one initial possibilities [i.e., the 30+11 described above], 22 colleagues agreed to participate. The ideal number of participants depends on the project as well as on the resources of the researcher. As there is no prescribed format for conducting a Delphi Study, there is also no prescribed ideal number of participants, although 5 to 10 people has been suggested to be an acceptable size of a homogeneous group (such as in this case, academics), and 15 to 40 people for a heterogeneous group of participants (Delbecq et al., 1975). Since the initial questions are traditionally open questions, the researcher has to be able to handle a considerable amount of information. The Delphi Study (3 rounds) was conducted between July and October 2010.

THE EXPERT PANEL

The first question in the Pre-Delphi Survey aimed to confirm that the participants are experts in intercultural competence. All respondents fulfilled more than one of the given criteria:

- I have published in the field (14)
- I have designed teaching material related to intercultural competence (14)
- I have teaching experience in ICC (14)
- I have work experience in ICC (outside of the university, for example as intercultural trainer) (8)
- Other (please specify) (13)

The additional answers under "other, please specify" indicated that participants had worked across multiple cultural contexts as diplomat, international office administration staff and intercultural trainer. Work experience covered business experience in multicultural teams, developing relationships between Indigenous Communities and MQ Faculty, organizing a workshop for overseas returnees in Tokyo and longstanding professional involvement in intercultural music performance. Decades of teaching international students was mentioned several times, also teaching on issues of anti-racism and related issues of diversity and social justice, teaching Indigenous History as a unit on the history of intercultural relations. Participants pointed out their research on international students and intercultural relationships and their experience in supervising Masters research and PhD theses on cultural issues. One participant was a faculty representative on the University Ethics committee which has involved reviewing a wide variety of applications covering a wide variety of contexts including projects dealing with aspects of intercultural relations/communication; another was a non-judicial member of the Equal Opportunity Division of the NSW Administrative Decisions Tribunal between 1996 and 2007.

Respondents were then asked about their own cultural background which most participants answered with their nationality.

- 5 participants identified themselves as Anglo-Australian, white Australian or Anglo-Celtic Australian
- 1 participant said s/he was European. Other Europeans are German, Polish, English, Scottish, and Finnish.
- One participant is Japanese, another Indian.
- 1 participant combined nationality with "Jewish", another has European and Australian citizenship, and one is "Anglophone Australian of Asian origin". Two participants describe themselves as "Celtic" or of "Anglo-Celtic" descent. One participant claims to be "culturally and linguistically diverse (CALD)"

It was the aim of this study to have an expert panel that consisted of male and female members from across all faculties and from various disciplines and that reflected a diverse mix of linguistic and cultural backgrounds. Most important though was the competence of the panel so that informed opinions could be collected, analyzed and ranked in order to come to an acceptable definition of intercultural competence at Macquarie, and to give some guidelines of how intercultural competence can be further developed.

Of the 22 experts, only 5 were male. Most participants were European and there was only one participant from the Science faculty. The strongest discipline in terms of participants was Linguistics. This uneven distribution may be due to various factors, such as that people in the Arts and Human Sciences work more closely with the concept of intercultural competence, especially if they are specializing in language and communication and human behaviour. The gender distribution is also not surprising and became even more obvious in the student survey. Language and intercultural skills seem to be more important to women than men.

OPINIONS EXPRESSED
IN THE PRE-DELPHI ROUND

The respondents were asked which intercultural skills students should develop at MQ and then how intercultural competence could be included in undergraduate and postgraduate curricula. The answers to the first question gave a first insight into their interpretation of intercultural competence, while those to the latter spread across a range of possibilities about how and where to include teaching intercultural competence, and how to support this teaching. The answers reflect 5 main ideas:

1. **Teaching intercultural competence across the curriculum:**
   - *People units* (designated units that focus on the challenges of contemporary society and to what it means to be ethical, local and global citizens)
   - Core of *capstone units* (final year units that consolidate learning and have many of the graduate capabilities and participation requirements embedded in them)
   - Lectures, seminars and tutorials that explicitly address the questions above
   - Incorporate aspects into general teaching
   - Mainstream it into as many units as possible
   - Introduction to other cultures/languages as part of the curriculum
   - Incorporate as part of graduate capabilities
   - Undertaking critical thinking and literacy in relation to media/communication/cultural studies units
   - Principles associated with intercultural competence should underpin and be integrated in all learning experience
   - Opportunities to intersect across cultures and the insertion of intercultural experiences and viewpoints across the curriculum

2. **Learning experiences in and out of the University**

   - Encourage students to participate in activities that expose them to the widest possible gamut of different cultural and social experiences,

both within the university and by participating in volunteer activities outside the university
- More focus on working with students to develop the competencies to present/do assignments with students from diverse cultural backgrounds
- Practical interaction between cultures at an everyday level
- Students to explore own cultural identity
- Showcase Macquarie's cultural diversity on the websites
- Cross-cultural mentoring teams
- Survival kits/docs

3. Guest speakers
- Regular guest speakers who can speak from own experience and budget earmarked for this within departments
- Guest speakers from a range of cultural backgrounds
- Invite speakers from representative communities
- Open house where experts from different cultures are invited and share the challenges they faced

4. Workshops, internships, projects
- Support and funding for students to organize their own activities exploring the above questions
- Projects which ensure that students from different cultures engage with each other in joint enterprises that are focused and facilitate mutual learning
- Culture sensitization workshops/Attendance of intercultural workshops
- Internship opportunities with consulate offices of different countries
- Opportunities to partner with immigration organizations that provide settlement services
- Show the variety of methodologies that do and do not work when working interculturally

5. Suggestions on how to teach and assess intercultural competence
- Small group exercises, role plays and debates around issues of intercultural competence
- Set short articles or videos as the basis of group discussions
- Small group work on multiple intercultural competence related topics and short presentations on them

- Presentations of situations which reconstruct intercultural misunderstanding and or tension for which students must suggest pathways of resolution
- Formulation of assessment tasks (questions, essays, short-story writing, report writing, journal entry targeted to questions of intercultural competence)
- Cross-cultural teamwork for some assignments with opportunities for students to reflect on cross-cultural issues and dynamics
- Exposure to key concepts on cultural diversity, cross-cultural communication, stereotyping, social identity theory
- Leaning experience that involves consideration of diverse cultures should endeavour to engage students in rich, meaningful exploration of cultural contexts
- Through constructing challenging situations that require students to question their own cultural values, assumptions and perspectives
- Multiple perspectives on content/issues to be learnt/discussed
- Give people vignettes to reveal how much they know/don't know, what their assumptions are
- Explain what xenophobia and ethnocentrism mean, but also warn that xenophilia and romanticism have their problems too

Most participants were unsure if students' intercultural competence should be assessed or not. Eleven participants were not sure, 6 said no and only 4 said yes. The word "competence" implies that it is a skill that can be measured and most participants feel unsure about the how and even more about why it should be measured by any standard set of criteria. One participant answered "no", but then said self-assessment would be useful, which is in line with another participant's answer that it is more important to provide students with genuine insights rather than have them repeat key phrases.

The BusinessDictionary (available from: http://www.businessdictionary .com/definition/competence.html) defines *competence* as a "cluster of related abilities, commitments, knowledge, and skills that enable a person (or an organization) to act effectively in a job or situation". The term *competency* is defined as "a cluster of abilities relating to excellence in a specific activity, [while] *competence* indicates sufficiency (state of being "good enough") of knowledge and skills that enable one to act in a wide variety of situations". In the context of intercultural competence this definition is particularly useful because it also refers to competence as something relative: "Because each level of responsibility has its own requirements, competence can occur in any period of a person's life or at any stage of his or her career". This issue will be deeper explored in the Delphi study.

Do you think students' intercultural competence should be assessed?

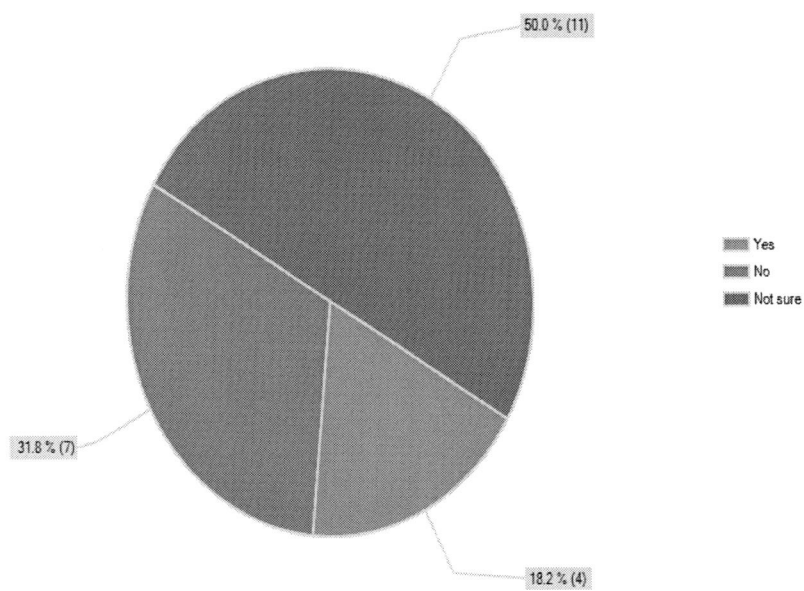

Fig. 2-1 Should students' intercultural competence be assessed?

THE DELPHI STUDY:
DELPHI ROUND 1

The first Delphi round consisted of 2 open questions:

- What constitutes intercultural competence?
- How can intercultural competence best be measured?

Both questions provided an open box for detailed answers. Twenty one of the 22 identified experts who had agreed to participate in the project answered the questions. The following is a representative answer to the first question:

> Generally that is related to respect for people from different cultures and any number of differences of identity. Appreciation of one's own cultural norms and assumptions, a capacity for empathy..., an ability to see beyond rigid social and cultural categories and to appreciate that different cultures are linked to different languages and styles of communication. Acceptance of ambiguity would represent a higher order competence.

While the first question generated quite a few similar answers and many ideas of what the term consists of, the second question divided the group into those who assume intercultural competence can be assessed and those who categorically reject measurement.

It was suggested that "Intercultural competence can best be measured by placing the individual who is tested in several different cultural groups in a lab experiment and subsequently asking members of the groups for assessments". Most participants introduced their answers by pointing out that "it is a difficult aspect of behaviour" or that they "feel uncomfortable about this question because ...we don't know what we would expect students to be able to do to demonstrate it". A couple of participants reject the idea altogether: "I think it's pointless to try and measure intercultural competence. Proficiency in another language is a pretty good indicator though [...]". All participants seemed to agree that, while desirable, measuring intercultural competence is a great challenge.

All answers to the two questions were sorted into clusters to produce a questionnaire for round 2 in which the participants were asked to rank each item. A six step Likert-type scale (strongly agree, agree, somewhat agree, somewhat disagree, disagree, strongly disagree) was used so that participants had to decide whether they are leaning towards agreement or disagreement.

DELPHI ROUND 2+3

The panel's input from round 1 produced 129 items to be rated. The first set of clusters (Definition, Awareness and Attitude, Knowledge and Comprehension, Skills and Competencies, Development and Outcomes) reflected the answers to "what constitutes intercultural competence". The second set of clusters (Measuring Intercultural Competence, Developing Tools for Measuring Intercultural Competence, Ways of Measuring, Intercultural Competence Components that can be measured) itemized the answers on how it could best be measured. Each set of questions was followed by an optional comment box for participants to suggest changes or to add items.

Some of the answers to the questionnaires will be reflected as graphs. The tables show the items the panel agreed on. Consensus was defined *a priori* to be >85% of members agreeing with an individual statement (strongly agree/agree), a mean of less than 1.75 (on a scale from 1 to 6, strongly agree to strongly disagree) and a standard deviation of less than 0.9. If any one of these criteria was not met, the item was moved to round 3. If more criteria were not met, the items were discarded.

Delphi round 1 resulted in a few general statements about intercultural competence. In this first question of round 2, experts agreed that intercultural competence is not static, depends on situation and context and is an interactive process. The second statement was confirmed in round 3 (94.7% agree), as was the last statement (100%).

Table 2-1: General statements about IC

Accepted	Rejected	Mean	SD	Item
21	0	1.43	0.68	IC is not static
18	2	1.55	1.15*	IC is an interactive process
17	2	1.63	1.16*	IC depends on situation and context

*These numbers are not within the set criteria. The items were therefore moved to round 3.

The panel agreed on most items about awareness and attitude, knowledge and comprehension, skills and competencies that were generated in round 1. In the part about openness, "the ability to maintain a sense of openness towards others" was rated as most important (mean: 1.21) followed by "willingness to listen for difference" (mean: 1.53) and "interest in learning about and engaging with people from diverse cultures" (mean: 1.53).

Experts could not agree on the value of imagination. One participant explained: "Imagination is perhaps too broad and empathy is better in that it allows people to imaginatively place themselves in a new situation or culture".

Table 2-2: Openness

Accepted	Rejected	Mean	SD	Item
19	0	1.21	0.54	Ability to maintain a sense of openness towards others
19	0	1.74	0.81	Interest to acquire knowledge of a new culture
19	0	1.68	0.67	Questioning and curiosity of practices and systems of belief
19	0	1.53	0.77	Willingness to listen for difference
18	1	1.53	0.84	Interest in learning about and engaging with people from diverse cultures

b) awareness/attitude

Most items regarding the importance of awareness as part of intercultural competence reached consensus in round 2. "Awareness of one's own and other cultures as points of reference for creating cultural identities" was ranked highest. "Self-awareness" was agreed on by 90% in round 3.

Table 2-3: Awareness

Accepted	Rejected	Mean	SD	Item
19	0	1.42	0.61	Awareness of one's own and other cultures as points of reference for creating cultural identities
20	1	1.81	0.81	Self-awareness
19	0	1.47	0.61	Appreciation of one's own cultural norms and assumptions
18	0	1.5	0.62	Sensitivity towards cultural difference and its effects on intercultural interaction, dialogue and communal living
18	1	1.74	0.87	Awareness of potential challenges and readiness to cope with them

c) Respect

Regarding the issue of *respect*, the panel differentiated between "respect for people from different cultures", "respect for differences of identity" and "respectful interaction with individuals whose ethnic and cultural backgrounds are different from your own". Each item reached consensus in round 2 with means around 1.5 and SDs of 0.83.

Table 2-4: Respect

Accepted	Rejected	Mean	SD	Item
19	1	1.55	0.83	Respect for people from different cultures
19	1	1.5	0.83	Respect for differences of identity
18	1	1.42	0.84	Respectful interaction with individuals whose ethnic and cultural backgrounds are different from our own
18	2	1.6	0.62	Being inclusive

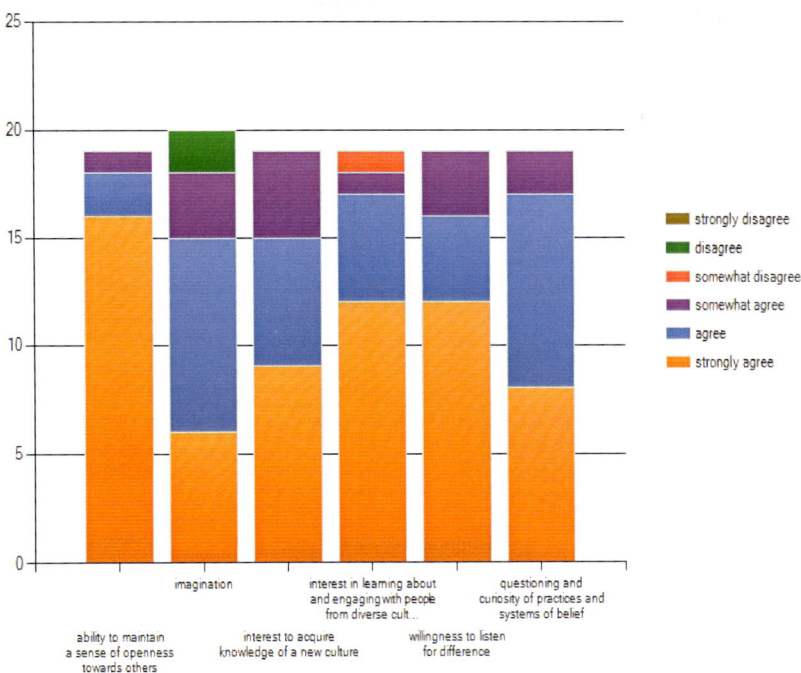

Fig. 2-2 Openness

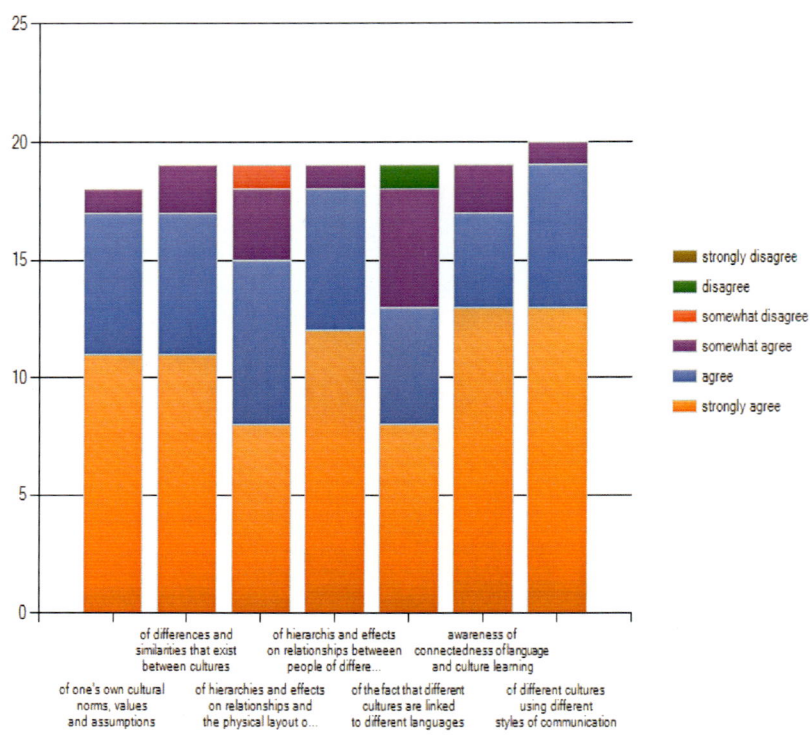

Fig. 2-3 Appreciation

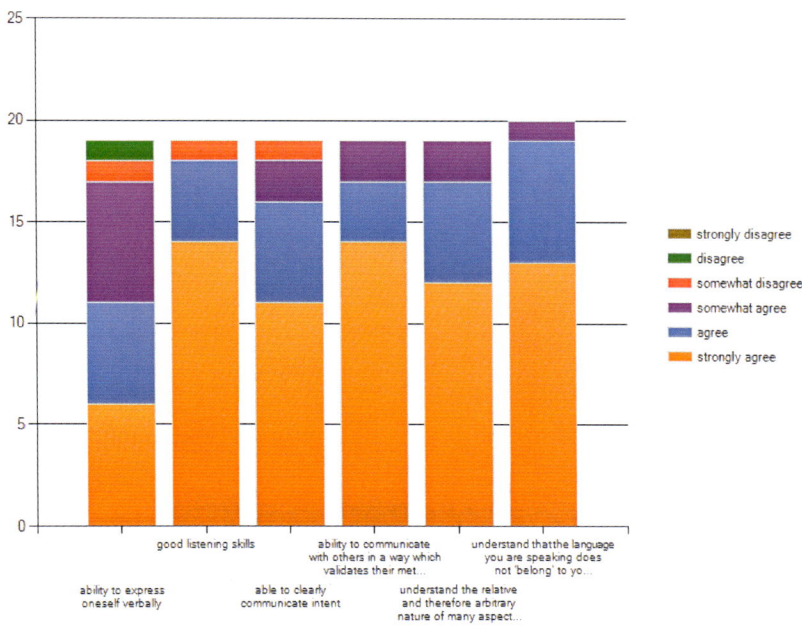

Fig. 2-4 Communication Skills

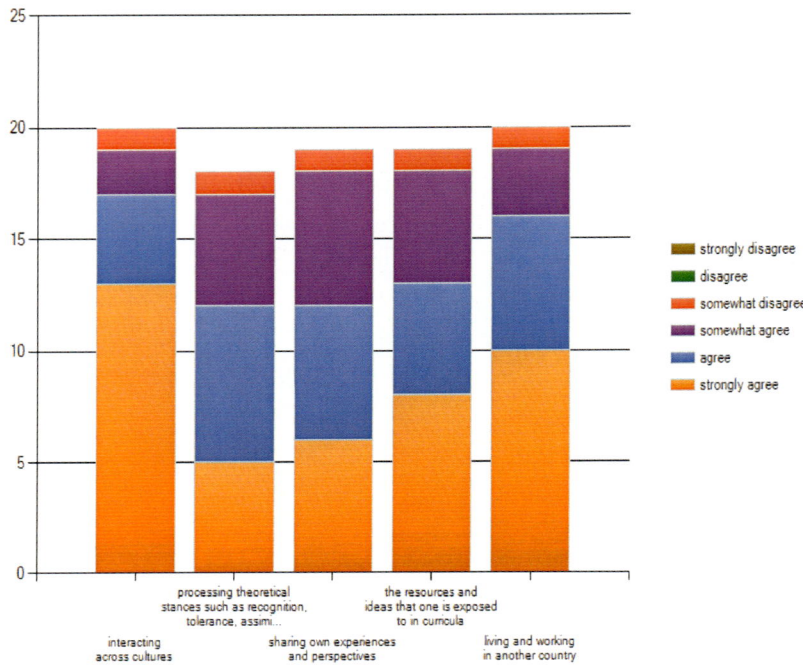

Fig. 2-5 Which intercultural skills can be developed?

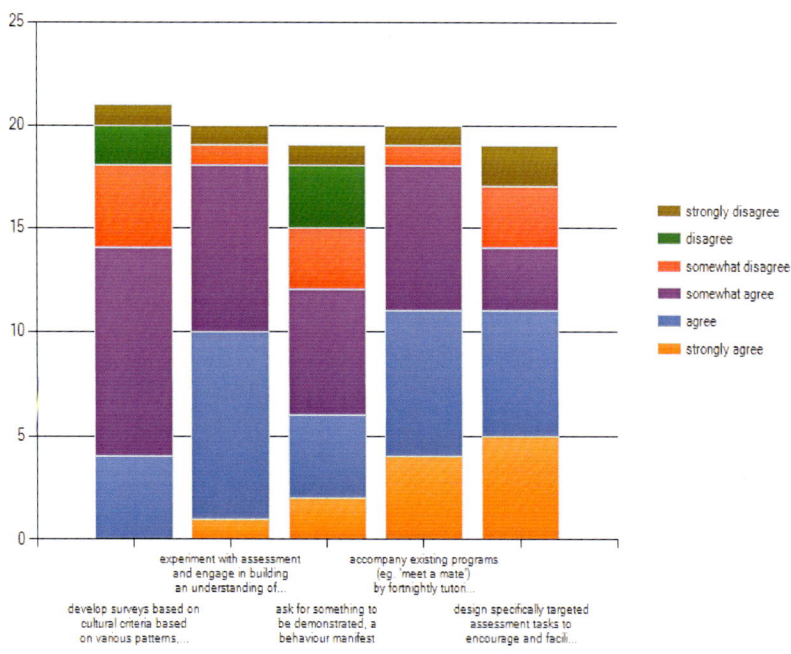

Fig. 2-6 How do we develop IC

The panel also agreed on most items about "appreciation" that were generated in round one, such as the appreciation of different cultures using different styles of communication (mean: 1.4), of hierarchies and effects on relationships between people of different socio-economic status and ages (mean: 1.42), and a general awareness of differences and similarities that exist between cultures (mean: 1.53). They agreed that intercultural competence includes "an awareness of connectedness of language and culture learning" (mean: 1.42).

Table 2-5: Appreciation

Accepted	Rejected	Mean	SD	Item
20	0	1.40	0.6	Of different cultures using different styles of communication
19	0	1.42	0.61	Of hierarchies and effects on relationships between people of different socio-economic status and ages
19	0	1.42	0.69	Awareness of connectedness of language and culture learning
19	0	1.53	0.7	Of differences and similarities that exist between cultures
18	0	1.44	0.62	Of one's own cultural norms, values and assumptions

b) Knowledge and Understanding

Round 1 generated a range of suggestions that were itemised under Knowledge and understanding in round 2. Participants agreed that "knowledge of culturally appropriate behaviour" is an important part of intercultural competence, but "knowledge of when to seek advice and where on matters of cultural difference" was rated as even more important. Other items did not achieve consensus.

Table 2-6: Knowledge and understanding

Accepted	Rejected	Mean	SD	Item
19	1	1.7	0.92	Of culturally appropriate behaviours
19	0	1.47	0.7	Of when to seek advice and where on matters of cultural difference

The next set of questions was around skills and competences. With the exception of "personal relaxation skills" (mean 2.84) all of the items under *basic skills* reached consensus:

Table 2-7: Basic IC skills

Accepted	Rejected	Mean	SD	Item
21	0	1.33	0.48	Ability to see beyond rigid social and cultural categories
19	1	1.50	0.76	Capacity for empathy for others
19	1	1.55	0.76	Ability to decentre and take up the perspective of the reader/listener
19	1	1.4	0.75	Ability to accept and respect differences without stereotyping or "othering" people or cultures
18	1	1.47	0.84	Ability to implement knowledge of a new culture in new environment

A range of communication skills was generated in round 1. Participants reached consensus on most of them in round 2 (see table below) and added the importance of non-verbal communication. This new item, "non-verbal skills are at least as important as verbal skills - good verbal skills don't always result in good communication" reached 100% in round 3. As reflected in the table below, communication skills include listening skills as well as the ability to communicate intent, but there was also a concern for communication styles and issues around ownership of language.

Table 2-8: Communication skills

Accepted	Rejected	Mean	SD	Item
20	0	1.4	0.6	Understand that the language you are speaking does not "belong" to you alone, but also to speakers who come to it with different values and assumptions which are reflected in their communication style
19	0	1.47	0.7	Understand the relative and therefore arbitrary nature of many aspects of communication that native speakers of a language may take for granted and take as axiomatic or "true"
18	1	1.37	0.76	Good listening skills
18	1	1.63	0.9	Able to clearly communicate intent
18	1	1.37	0.68	Ability to communicate with others in a way which validates their method of communication, mode of speech and level of understanding

Three items were listed under the heading *higher order competencies* (heading suggested by a participant). The ability to accept ambiguity was strongly agreed/agreed on by all participants. They also reached consensus about the ability to establish and maintain relationships (94.7% in round 3).

Table 2-9: Higher order competencies

Accepted	Rejected	Mean	SD	Item
20	0	1.35	0.49	Ability to accept ambiguity
18	2	1.75	0.97*	Ability to establish and maintain relationships

*This number is not within the set criteria. The item was therefore moved to round 3.

While the definition of intercultural competence and agreement on skills and knowledge that an interculturally competent person needs to develop seemed to be an easy task, it was seen as less obvious how this goal can be achieved and how an increase in intercultural competence could be measured or assessed.

Participants agreed on two items (the second one in round 3, 94.7%) to best develop intercultural competence. The other 3 items were discarded for lack of consensus.

Table 2-10: How to develop IC

Accepted	Rejected	Mean	SD	Item
18	1	1.79	0.89	Interacting across cultures
19	1	1.75	0.91*	Living and working in another country

*This number is not within the set criteria. The item was therefore moved to round 3.

The panel agreed on the four abilities reflected in the table below that characterise an interculturally competent person. Six other items were moved to round 3 of the study and some of them reached consensus. In the last round, the panel agreed that interculturally competent people "are able to adapt their own behaviour" (88.9%), "make individuals and groups of another culture to feel [their] respect for their culture" (89.5%), "deconstruct stereotypes and preconceptions" (94.4%), and "reduce intolerance" (94.7%).

Table 2-11: Skills of interculturally competent people

Accepted	Rejected	Mean	SD	Item
20	0	1.6	0.68	Negotiate and move between and across complex cultural domains
18	1	1.47	0.77	Engage in meaningful ways with people across cultures
19	1	1.7	0.86	Operate effectively in other cultures
19	0	1.53	0.7	Smooth intercultural exchange where neither participant feels they're the misunderstood participant, and neither feels the burden of adaptations falls to them

The results on how to measure intercultural competence were very different from the results about its nature. This is not surprising, taking into account that only 4 participants expressed in the pre Delphi Survey that they were confident about measuring intercultural competence while 11 of them were not sure and 7 rejected measuring altogether. Nevertheless, the first round generated many suggestions about what can possibly be measured and how to go about it, though there were a couple of experts who did not provide any answers because they oppose the idea. When the items were in clusters and rated, only a few were agreed upon by the expert panel and those mainly related to the kind of problems involved with measuring. One participant commented that it is difficult to agree to a method of measuring without knowing more about the context, e.g. who is being assessed and why is intercultural competence being measured. The following tables show the items panel members agreed on.

Table 2-12: How intercultural competence should be measured depends on

Accepted	Rejected	Mean	SD	Item
19	0	1.37	0.5	The definition of intercultural competence
18	1	1.63	0.9	Why and where you are assessing

The next question, "How much do you agree or disagree with the following opinions about measuring intercultural communicative competence", only leads to one agreement: Measuring ICC is challenging.

Table 2-13: Measuring IC

Accepted	Rejected	Mean	SD	Item
18	1	1.53	0.84	Measuring ICC is challenging

Two statements were included in Delphi round 3 because they almost reached consensus, "ICC should not be measured for the sake of it" and "The notion of competence in any field is directly related to the specific context in which something occurs". Only the latter item was agreed on in round 3 (100%) The panel could not agree on statements expressing that measuring intercultural competence is meaningless, unreliable or ineffective *per se*. Therefore, all other items (7) were discarded (high standard deviation and means around 3.0).

In this part of the survey, the way the data is interpreted is very important. Summarising all answers under "strongly agree", "agree" or "somewhat agree" as "agree" would lead to results that suggest agreement among experts. If only the first options, strongly agree and agree are combined, the result is a different one. Together with the mean and considering SD, the results suggest that there is no strong agreement among the 21 experts. Comparing the relative agreement levels to the consensus achieved in the first part of the survey where experts rate the ingredients of intercultural competence, there is a significant difference. Under the rules set *a priori* to the whole survey, the panel also rejected all items on how to develop intercultural communicative competence that were generated in round 1.

Round 1 also resulted in a short list of indicators of intercultural communicative competence. The rating of these items was very mixed, "proficiency in another language", for example, reached an average rating of 2.9 and a standard deviation of 1.37. In Byram's view (1997), language proficiency is central to intercultural communicative competence. Gudykunst (1991, p. 2), on the other hand, points out that "If we understand each others' languages, but not their cultures, we can make fluent fools of ourselves". Language proficiency was pointed out as an important aspect of intercultural competence in the internationalization survey as well as in the pre-Delphi round. It is important to note that in this study, knowledge of a foreign language is seen as central and inseparable from cultural knowledge.

Two items, "the ability to demonstrate appropriate behaviour in real life" and "If there is a negotiation of any difference in understanding and ways of doing things" were transferred to round 3 because they were close to agreement. Both reached agreement (94.1%) in the last round. Other items were discarded.

In round 1, a fairly long list of possible ways of measuring intercultural competence was generated by the expert panel. One participant pointed out that measurement needs to be suitable to situation and context, which means it is difficult to rate which measurement is best from a list of available techniques. All but one participant of the Delphi panel at Macquarie agreed that "Any one measurement won't be enough to assess intercultural communicative competence" (mean 1.95). To come to any meaningful conclusion about a person's intercultural competence, a set of measuring tool needs to be employed. Deardorff (2009, p. 486) lists "using only one tool or method to assess intercultural competence" as one of the pitfalls in assessing intercultural competence and advocates "[...] a multi-method, multi-perspective assessment package [...]." The panel pointed out another problem that evolves when measuring intercultural communicative competence: "There is considerable political correctness associated with ICC, questionnaires can therefore be fudged because people critically appraise their responses according to a pc filter" (mean: 1.75).

Though none of the items reached agreement, it will be interesting to have a look at the suggestions and how they were rated. The following table shows how the items were rated in the order from the highest to the lowest mean. To interview participants who are involved in working in culturally diverse settings was rated as strongly agree and agree by 80% of the participants. For all other items most experts tended to "somewhat agree".

Table 2-14: Methods of assessing Intercultural Competence

Accepted	Rejected	Mean	SD	Item
17	2	2.16	1.01	Qualitative self-reflective data
18	**2**	**2.20**	**1.28**	**Interview participants who are involved in working in culturally diverse settings**
18	1	2.21	0.98	Learner diaries (e.g. semester abroad)
16	3	2.32	1.38	Peer observation
17	4	2.33	1.59	Observation of unguarded interactions between culturally different persons
17	3	2.35	1.46	Observation
18	1	2.47	0.96	Student feedback (in a uni situation)
18	3	2.57	1.36	Interviews
17	3	2.75	1.07	Role plays
16	4	2.85	1.27	Experiment with various assessments
16	4	2.90	1.25	Self-reporting
11	6	2.94	1.68	In vivo
10	7	3.24	1.35	Surveys of people from other cultures that learners deal with
13	8	3.38	1.20	Surveys
8	10	3.72	1.41	Reputation
6	15	4.05	1.6	By placing the individual who is tested in several different cultural groups in a lab experiment and subsequently asking members of the groups for assessments

The panel did agree on potential problems of measuring intercultural competence:

Table 2-15: Problems in assessing IC

Accepted	Rejected	Mean	SD	Item
20	0	1.75	0.72	There is considerable political correctness associated with ICC, questionnaires can therefore be fudged because people critically appraise their responses according to a pc filter
18	1	1.95	0.69	Any one measurement won't be enough to assess intercultural communicative competence

Two items, "multiple choice tests or similar approaches use a simplified approach resulting in general statements or relying on the assumptions of homogenous cultures and societies" and "measurements of such complex issues stands in danger of being stereotypical in its own right" were almost agreed on and therefore moved to round 3. Both items reached agreement (95% and 90% respectively)

The last list of items in Delphi round 2 consisted of a list of items relating to intercultural competence, asking the panel if they can be measured or not. The following table shows the items ranked by mean. Though it seems that the majority of participants agree on many items, there was no agreement that matched the set agreement criteria. This is due to very few participants choosing "strongly agree" or "agree", but rather "somewhat agree" which in this study is not enough to qualify as agreement.

Table 2-16: Measurable parts of IC

Accepted	Rejected	Mean	SD	Item
17	1	2.06	1.11	Individual's willingness to engage with people from other cultures
17	1	2.06	1.11	Readiness to communicate even if by using unfamiliar language and communication patterns
17	1	2.17	1.10	Openness to participate in the activities in new environment
16	2	2.22	1.11	Components such as adaptability, risk taking, sensitivity to cultural differences, ability to initiate interaction
16	2	2.39	1.09	Extent to which people feel like equal participants in groups, do they feel listened to, do they feel that they are able to participate verbally, do they feel respected etc.
15	3	2.44	1.09	The extent to which individuals can acknowledge and reflect on the unique lenses through which they are likely to interpret interactions and experiences
16	2	2.44	1.1	Understanding of the goals/project being discussed within culturally diverse groups
15	3	2.50	1.04	The extent to which individuals are able to adapt to contexts with which they are unfamiliar
14	4	2.56	1.1	The degree and seriousness of examples of miscommunication and the ability to successfully repair such breakdowns
15	3	2.61	1.14	Degree of comfort an individual displays in interacting with others from a different culture
12	6	2.72	1.27	Ability not to stereotype

DELPHI ROUND 3

Statements that reached consensus at the end of round 2 were not reiterated in round 3. Round 3 included questions in which consensus was not quite reached as well as new statements derived from comments in round 2 for the panel to agree or disagree to. Twenty one new items were included in this questionnaire, most of them being variations of items rated in round 2. The expert panel agreed (85%-100%) on 5 new items.

They decided that intercultural competence relies on the "willingness to listen, to hear and to recognise the emotional, social and cultural relevance/s of difference", and agreed that "self-awareness and what it means in terms of your own cultural positioning and human needs" is an important prerequisite to intercultural competence. "Willingness to listen for difference" can be interpreted as an expectancy of otherness which has negative impact on intercultural encounters, but it can also mean an awareness of where social conventions differ. An ignorance of cultural differences may lead to unintended taboo violations, especially where taboo and silence are combined and used as tools. To avoid a breakdown in communication, it is important to be aware of the culture specific meanings of these terms (Krajewski and Schröder, 2009).

Additional important skills are "increased awareness of existing stereotypes and of how they can affect responses and behaviour" as well as non-verbal skills which are "at least as important as verbal skills". The only additional idea about measuring intercultural communicative competence that the panel agreed on is that "tutorials could cover some aspects of IC (e.g. social/spatial/hierarchical differences) and within that context get students to reflect on their intercultural experiences".

To summarise, then, the study exemplifies that experts in intercultural communication agree on the main ingredients of intercultural competence and stress attitudes such as openness and genuine interest in people from other cultures. Empathy and the ability to see an issue from various angles is rated as one of the most important skills for people to successfully relate to others. This was, in fact, the only item agreed upon 100% by the top ICC scholars in the Deardorff study. Most of the items generated in round 1 of the Delphi Study reflect awareness, knowledge and skills that contribute to deconstructing the division between in-group and out-group and thereby lead to *identity inclusivity*. Kim (2009) summarizes this inclusivity as a central issue of intercultural competence: "The more inclusive an individual's identity orientation, the greater his or her capacity to engage in cooperative intercultural relationships". The second theorem she introduces in her article is about *identity security* which refers to the level of strength an individual may draw upon in stressful situations such as cultural transitions: "The more secure an individual's identity orientation, the greater his or her capacity to engage in cooperative intercultural relationships". This is reflected in "the appreciation of one's own cultural norms and assumptions" which was seen as of vital importance in this study.

CHAPTER THREE:

THE STUDENT VOICE

We live in a postmodern world, where everything is possible and almost nothing is certain.... The planetary civilization to which we all belong confronts us with global challenges. We stand helpless before them because our civilization has essentially globalized only the surface of our lives. But our inner self continues to have a life of its own. And the fewer answers the era of rational knowledge provides to the basic questions of human being, the more deeply it would seem that people, behind its back as it were, cling to the ancient certainties of their tribe.
—Vaclav Havel, Former President of the Czech Republic Speech at Independence Hall, July 4, 1994

STUDENT PARTICIPANTS

This project set out to explore the importance of intercultural competence at Macquarie University by means of a Delphi Study with experts among Macquarie staff and by distributing a questionnaire among students across faculties. Unlike the Delphi study, the student questionnaire does not aim at consensus but at getting an idea about how students feel about intercultural competence and in particular about intercultural competence as a graduate capability.

To address a wide range of students, a random selection of classes that were running in semester 2, 2010, was made. To arrive at a manageable sample size and address classes across all disciplines, selection was narrowed down to classes for students in their second and fourth year of undergraduate study only. A total of 37 undergraduate classes and 15 postgraduate classes were identified from the course handbooks. Convenors were contacted by email and asked to invite their students to our survey and to place the survey link onto their web-based teaching blackboards. Some colleagues invited us to introduce our survey and hand out hard copies of the questionnaire. As an incentive to participate in the survey, students were offered to enter a prize draw at the end of the survey where they could win one of four gift vouchers worth A$25 each. Though the response rate via a survey monkey link on blackboards is generally low, a total of 208 questionnaires were filled in. Taking into account that class size varied from 6 students to over 40, the response rate is somewhere between 15-20%.

It can be assumed that the online questionnaire was answered by students who were curious about the topic. The results show that most of the participants are aware of the concept and related research; they use appropriate terminology or cite relevant scholars. The hard copy version had the advantage that usually all students present did fill it in during our visit, so it includes the opinions of students who would probably not have completed the online version. The numbers of female (75.6%) and male students (24.4%) who took the survey suggest that intercultural competence is seen as a soft skill and a rather "female topic". In one of the smaller classes in which the paper version was conducted, the only male student chose not to participate in the survey while the seven female students completed it. The questionnaire also asked students to express their interest in participating in a focus group at a later stage. About 23% (46) of the participants did so; all but two of them were female.

Most students who took the questionnaire were aged between 20 and 25 years old (55%). Because we also asked postgraduate students to participate, ages ranged from under 20 to over 35. Ninety-six students were enrolled for a Bachelor degree, 105 for a Masters and 5 are PhD candidates. Most students who took the online version are from the Faculty of Arts. It can be assumed that many of the students from the Arts Faculty and Human Sciences come across various concepts of intercultural competence during their studies, especially if they are involved in fields such as linguistics or communications. Participants came from a variety of disciplines such as psychology, biochemistry, applied finance, international studies, international relations, sustainable development, French, ancient history, marketing, international communication, wildlife conservation, early childhood education, environmental education, applied linguistics, economics, statistics, translating and interpreting, and social health.

Table 3-1: Participating students by faculty

Faculty	No of Students in sample
Faculty of Arts	80
Faculty of Human Sciences	42
Faculty of Business and Economics	38
Faculty of Science	29

Note: The remaining students in the sample did not identify their faculty.

Students were asked about their cultural backgrounds and to indicate their mother tongue and any other languages they speak. Maybe it is not a surprise that more international students than domestic students were participating in our project, though the notion that intercultural competence is more important for international than Australian students was clearly rejected by international as well as Australian participants.

Table 3-2: Participants by cultural background

Cultural Background	No of Students in Sample
Australian	50
Asian	46
Chinese	29
European	23
Other	22
US American	11

Note: Not all students in the sample identified their cultural background

Students grouped as Asian are from Malaysia, the Philippines, India, Korea, Taiwan, Japan, Vietnam, Thailand and Bangladesh. The European group consists of students from Italy, Hungary, Serbia, Germany, the Netherlands, Denmark, England, Ireland, as well as those who identified themselves as *European*. Other students are from Africa, Turkey, Mexico, Paraguay, Saudi Arabia, and Egypt. One student identifies as Indo-Fijian/New Zealander.

STUDENT SURVEY RESULTS

The student survey consists of 3 parts; the first is asking participants to rank how much they agree with statements around intercultural competence, the second is asking for their opinion on the importance of suggested ingredients of intercultural competence and the last part is about themselves and their backgrounds. Each set of questions was followed by an open box for additional comments. In the end students can volunteer as prospective participants of focus groups and leave their email addresses if they want to participate in a prize draw.

Students were asked to rate each of the following statements on a scale from 1 (fully agree) to 6 (completely disagree). The items in the following table have been sorted from lowest to highest mean.

Most students (95.6%) agreed or strongly agreed to the first statement: "It is important to be able to get along with people from other culture". More than half of the participating students (57.7%) claim to "sometimes find it difficult to interact with people from other cultural and linguistic backgrounds".

Students do not think that "there are already enough programs at uni about intercultural skills". 41.7% somewhat disagree and 23.4% disagree and strongly disagree with this statement. The opposite statement "There is a need for more extracurricular workshops about intercultural competencies" was agreed to or strongly agreed to by 37.8%, and somewhat agreed to by 40.2% of students. 49.4% of our participants said that they would attend extracurricular workshops to gain intercultural skills and 53.1% would like to see their intercultural skills accredited in some way. Looking at individual questionnaires though, these were not necessarily the same students.

The majority agree that "Intercultural competencies should be an integral part of as many classes as possible" (44.9% agree or strongly agree, an additional 32.7% somewhat agree). The statement "classes are so diverse that I automatically gain intercultural competence" was agreed to or strongly agreed to by 29.9%. An additional 39.2% said that they somewhat agree.

Table 3-3: IC related statements

ITEM	Mean
It is important to be able to get along with people from other cultures	1.38
It is important to know one's own cultural background in order to have good interaction with students from other cultures	2.29
There should be more training for staff about how to cater to internationalised student groups	2.4
Intercultural Competence should be a graduate capability at MQ	2.42
I would like to have some sort of certificate about my intercultural skills when I graduate	2.59
Intercultural competencies should be an integral part of as many classes as possible	2.67
There is a need for more extracurricular workshops about intercultural competencies	2.76
I would be interested in attending extra-curricular workshops to gain intercultural skills	2.81
MQ classes are so diverse that I automatically gain intercultural competence	3.07
I sometimes find it difficult to interact with people from other cultural and linguistic backgrounds	3.44
Intercultural Competence is an extra skill that should not be a general graduate capability at MQ	3.79
There are already enough programs at MQ about intercultural skills	3.87
Intercultural skills are important but future employers are not interested in them	3.94
Intercultural Competence is more important for international students than for local students	4.08
Intercultural Competence is only important for people who plan to work in an international environment	4.6

55.3% of students agree or fully agree with the notion that "Intercultural Competence should be a graduate capability at university", while the reverse statement "Intercultural Competence is an extra skill that should not be a general graduate capability at uni" was rejected by 34.6% who disagree or strongly disagree and 23.3% who somewhat disagree.

Increasing intercultural competence is seen as an issue concerning students and staff alike: 86.7% of the respondents think that there should be more training for staff with 54.2% agreeing or strongly agreeing to the related statement.

The following three statements aimed at finding out whether students think of Intercultural Competence as more important for some groups than others. A total of 60.2% disagreed or strongly disagreed with the statement "Intercultural Competence is only important for people who plan to work in an international environment". Most students also disagreed with the statement "Intercultural skills are important but future employers are not interested in them" (36.6% disagree and strongly disagree, a further 27.8% somewhat disagree). The third statement, "Intercultural Competence is more important for international students than for local students" was rejected by 64.1% of students, but 21.4% agreed and strongly agreed. These numbers reflect answers of Australian and international students alike.

Some of the additional statements provided in the open textbox were

- Make sessions that count towards GLP (Global Leadership Program) credit perhaps?
- It is good to provide some workshops about religious cultures.
- ...globalisation has created the need for multicultural awareness and sensitivity. Many problems arise due to ignorance and could be solved simply through a better education of the population on the whole.
- How would you judge intercultural competencies? Rather than a course there should be more social encouragement!
- Intercultural sensitivity especially by lecturers in politics and history units

The second set of items refers to the components of intercultural competence. Students were asked to rate how important each issue is for successful communication with people from other cultures.

A total of 96.5% of student participants rank "respect" as the most important issue in intercultural communication. The term is very broad though and may mean anything between tolerance and acceptance; however, respect is seen as very important by 80%, tolerance by 60% of our participants. Foreign language skills were seen as important or very important by 58% of our students, most of these students speak several languages.

Some of the additional statements provided in the open textbox were

- Religious culture is important and quite sensitive, at the same time, some religious culture like Islam encourages Muslim to be opened...how can we get the advantage of religious culture?
- Frequent interaction
- I think self-understanding is very important, too...you do not have to cater to other cultures and people. Cultural diversity should not be a barrier for people at all...How much can you handle?

STUDENTS AND STAFF ON INTERCULTURAL COMPETENCE

The following is a list of comparable items about intercultural competence that were rated by staff and students. The means are close together in some instances (e.g. listening skills and other communication skills, respect, and empathy) but far from each other in others. "Awareness of my own culture" was seen as more important by the expert panel than by the student sample. Similarly the panel rates "knowledge of how other cultures work" as very important, while the students rate culture-specific knowledge as less relevant for intercultural competence. Both groups ranked "awareness of the language behind the culture" and "imagination" further down the list.

Table 3-4: Comparison Delphi/students

Item Delphi	Item student questionnaire	Mean Delphi	Mean student	Delphi Agree/ strongly agree	Students Important/ very important
Ability to maintain a sense of openness towards others	Openness	**1.21**	1.62	94.7%	88.5%
Good listening skills	Listening skills	1.37	1.43	94.8%	96%
Respectful interaction with individuals whose ethnic and cultural backgrounds are different from our own	Respect	1.42	**1.24**	89.5%	96.5%

Appreciation of one's own cultural norms and assumptions	Awareness of my own culture	1.47	2.19	94.7%	65.5%
Capacity for empathy for others	Empathy (ability to take the perspective of the other person)	1.5	1.6	95%	91%
Able to clearly communicate intent	Communication skills	1.63	1.36	94.2%	95.6%
Interest to acquire knowledge of a new culture	Curiosity (about other cultures)	1.74	2.06	79%	69.9%
Adapt one's own behaviour	Ability to adapt	1.79	1.63	73.7%	90%
Knowledge of how other cultures work	Culture-specific knowledge	1.84	2.41	79%	61.3%
Appreciation of the fact that different culture are linked to different languages	Awareness of the language behind the culture	2.00	2.33	68.4%	60.5%
Imagination	Imagination	2.15	2.58	75%	49%

OPEN QUESTIONS

Students were asked to complete two statements: "To me, internationalization at university means..." and "I think the most important things about intercultural communication and intercultural competence are..."

Students amalgamated the questions and answered them in similar ways. For most students in my sample internationalization at university is directly relating to their everyday lives, it means "...students from different cultural backgrounds", "... to encounter and interact with other nationalities and cultures every day in classes and on campus", and "acceptance and integration of different cultures".

Some of the answers are process oriented: Internationalization at uni is "the process of becoming aware of the diversity of cultures in university environment and being able to adapt to it", "developing awareness of international issues and culture among staff and students", "shift ... one's cultural point of view towards other culture, try to blend together with other culture and respect others from different culture... in some classes quite hard to achieve since lack of respect throughout different cultures, even in academic class environment or formal lecture and student situation"

Most students see the large international student population at university as an "incredible opportunity to interact with people from around the world which has made my experience here very rich". An international student felt there were not enough Australian students in her classes: "everyone on master level is international, wish there were more Australians so [I] can learn about Aussie culture, too".

Some students mentioned that "in some cases large international student groups from the same country tend to build their own in-groups, speaking their native language and not really interacting with students with other nationalities". This point was made by domestic students especially and rated negatively. On the other hand, a number of international students, especially from Asia, felt that their language skills were a barrier in interacting with domestic students or fluent English speakers as they would become impatient during conversations: "It's so difficult for me to understand the local people speaking. Slang and idiom is so difficult and lead to boring conversation. I have few Aussie friends".

The second statement was generally completed with the key components of intercultural competence that were given in the second part of the questionnaire. The four characteristics that were mentioned repeatedly are tolerance, respect, open-mindedness, and understanding. Understanding here referred to two different things, i.e. understanding in terms of language and communication and understanding in terms of empathy and compassion. Representative answers were: "respect, tolerance and dialogue", "the ability to learn from other cultures, new ways of thinking and perceiving the world", "empathy and the ability to listen, not judge". Language skills were an issue for many students: "language skills, sometime[s] I'm just shy to communicate with others because of my inconfidence of my English" [sic].

Many students indicated that interacting with students from different cultures can be a beneficial learning experience for both, domestic and international students. Some participants added the importance of knowing and being confident about one's own culture: "Openness, peaceful attitude and confidence of your identities". Students stressed that it is important "to understand each other, not necessarily to accept" and that "a respectful attitude on both sides, a willingness to listen, recognition of the need to learn, and a willingness to put aside hasty value judgements" is vital in intercultural communication.

STUDENT FOCUS GROUP

A focus group discussion with 6 students took place in October 2010 at MQ University. All 46 students who had filled in the survey and indicated interest in a focus group discussion were invited by email. The email included a fixed time and place as well as the key questions to be discussed. Some students had classes at the suggested time, others declined because they were too busy with assignments at this time of year. Six students agreed and came to the round table discussion which included a light lunch.

Participants were informed that the session would be recorded so that the researchers could concentrate on the participants instead of taking notes. All participants signed information and consent forms. Our participating students came from different faculties and personal backgrounds. The following information was provided by our participants when they completed the online student questionnaire.

- Kayten, postgraduate student from the Philippines.
  o Area of study: Sustainable Development, Faculty of Science
  o Finds it enriching to work with different cultures, plans walkabout in the Philippines

- Sue, postgraduate student from China
  o Area of study: International communication, Faculty of Arts
  o She studied English in China for 4 years and learned that "Language alone does not mean you can communicate well".

- Maria, postgraduate student with Italian-Spanish-Uruguayan background.
  o Area of study: Applied Linguistics, Faculty of Human Sciences
  o She is a teacher who works with students from all over the world. She has been living in Sydney with family since 2007.

- Grace, postgraduate student from Australia.
  o Area of study: Applied Linguistics, Faculty of Human Sciences
  o She studied at various other Australian universities and is a practising musician. Grace is working on a language teaching tool

on spoken language only and aims to produce a "universal utterances" video.

- Yousef, doctoral candidate from Saudi-Arabia.
  o Area of study: Diversity management. Faculty of Business and Economics
  o He came to Australia in 2007 with no English. He is now working on his PhD thesis on diversity management in the work place. His religious background is Islamic and he chose Sydney to raise his family. Yousef says that he enjoys the multicultural environment and never experienced culture shock.

- Kirsten, postgraduate student from Denmark.
  o Area of study: International Communication, Faculty of Arts
  o She has a BA in English and French business communication and started her MA in international communication to become a better HR manager.

After an introduction round, each participant in turn answered the first question:

Q1 What are the most important ingredients of intercultural competence, what constitutes intercultural competence?

Awareness and respect were identified as the most important issues which reflects the results of the questionnaire. Several participants mentioned "awareness of differences" as an important part of intercultural competence, also "patience" and "preparedness for intercultural encounters". Kirsten said that it is important to be able "to recognise that you are culturally biased".

To treat other people with respect and to value where people come from was agreed on as a skill. The group discussed what it means to actually understand the other. Sue pointed out: "You may be able to communicate in the same language but not necessarily understand what the other is really talking about". Understanding needs to go beyond language and knowledge of concepts such as low and high context cultures will be helpful. The group agreed that interconnectedness is there, but people need to be more considerate and value where people come from. Collaboration is possible if we communicate with understanding of and for other people. An example of different values and beliefs being expressed in different ways can be found in doctor/patient conversations, they need to understand each other beyond language.

Yousef pointed out that it is vital to "understand and respect other cultures", but "not necessarily accept" them. It is important to "maintain your own culture at the same time. In Saudi Arabia most people say: learn English before you go abroad. But to study culture would be very important; I wish I could have learned about the culture before I came".

We can communicate even though we speak different languages. Respect is vital, not necessarily acceptance. To prepare for another culture it is proposed to study theories, literature about the culture to get an idea about how it differs from one's own culture. Awareness of the new culture can be created by reading online materials such as blogs about the differences of life in one's own and in the host culture. Impressions may be stereotypical but to consider differences before travelling will be useful. In Saudi Arabia, Australia is seen as "the cute daughter of the UK" while Australians see their culture as distinct from the British.

Q2 What are the advantages of being interculturally competent?

This question was answered in general terms and discussed in the specific context of essay writing. In general, being able to communicate with other cultures brings more knowledge and results in less conflict: "There is less conflict if you are able to communicate with others", says Yousef, "In my country people have strong stereotypes towards some countries". He also stresses that it is important to have global characteristics to be able to work in different parts of the world. Multicultural persons can work anywhere, monocultural people cannot. Kayten explains that in the Philippines IC means more diversity. Influences from other cultures are good and a mix of 3 or more cultures together creates new perspectives. For Chinese, learning about and communicating with people from other cultures is important if they want to do business, says Sue. Kirsten agrees that IC eases business communication and avoids conflict. "Part of my personality is efficiency and IC speeds up the process so you don't waste time misunderstanding each other."

Grace, the only Australian and true Sydneysider in this round table discussion, points out the importance of the host culture in reaching mutual understanding: "IC for me means that I can make myself available to be helpful. (...) I present a friendly face. (...) I am aware of others and where they come from; I am open to the world and want to encourage [that]".

Participants discussed the example of different essay writing styles in different cultures. It was said that Western people start their essays differently, people in Saudi Arabia start with background information and historical views; people from China "start with the end". Intercultural competence should lead to acknowledgements of different orders and teaching staff should not insist on strict guidelines but be a bit more flexible.

Q 3 From your experience, how well is MQ staff prepared to teach international classes?

The group agreed that there is awareness about international backgrounds and MQ staff is in general well prepared to cater to international classes, but there are always "...some people (who) don't have that cultural awareness and they are pretty rude".

One participant said that in another university "some convenors force students to adapt and I had to write in Australian English, I was not allowed to write American English. They force us to adapt". When asked if they thought that intercultural competence should be a graduate capability at Macquarie, 3 participants said yes, the other 3 said no. During the discussion about this one participant changed her mind and agreed that it should be a graduate capability. The main argument against IC becoming a graduate capability for all students was that it is not of equal importance for all graduates to be interculturally competent: "For someone studying some subject that later takes him to work in a remote area in Australia, it is not important to become interculturally competent. For others it is a necessity".

Kayten argued that it is important for everyone to open their mind, "because once he is back in [Korea] he may work with people from elsewhere. It is necessary to develop "Awareness at least, maybe [it should] not [be] a graduate capability but at least a workshop would be good. Learning is not limited to formal settings, there are other ways and we all need to open our minds and need to build that capacity so that we have it when we need it". Learning is not about assessment, there are different scenarios.

The group also considered if people who are already culturally competent don't need any more training, but in the end they decided that "you never finish, it is an ongoing learning process". IC is important for everyone but not a priority for everyone.

Q 4 How do we get there, what approaches do increase awareness at MQ?

Kirsten summarised that intercultural awareness starts with a state of mind, openness. It is good to "expose people to different cultures, put them in situations". It was also agreed that reading relevant literature and studying case studies would be a good formal approach. It is important to read and to discuss, but also to share social events.

It was suggested that university members need to be inspired, inspiring speeches would encourage students and staff to increase their IC, "it is not something religious, but some people can give you inspiration". Kayten pointed out that "kitchen table discussions" are a useful approach because it is a good start for people to share food. "When we share it is an enriching experience, you take the talk about the food (and then about) history and culture."

Grace and Yousef emphasised the importance of working overseas, "in a very different culture, not from US to Canada but from Australia to Saudi Arabia, and for a longer period of time so you learn much". Yousef also said to read as much as you can, to learn something about cultural intelligence theory. The theory proposes to learn about a different culture, then try to behave like their culture, then try to think like people from that culture.

Maria explained how professional development sessions about different issues such as the use of smartboards can increase intercultural competence. "Everyone goes, you learn how to use the smartboard with people from different countries."

The group agreed that there should be awareness training in formal seminars but identified the problem that "you cannot force someone to do it. People who think they don't need it will not go to those".

The final result was that exchange programs are an important part of institutionalising IC, that theory and practice have to complement each other and that people need to be inspired to go to a workshop. "You will always get those who are aware and open anyway." To reach others, you need to "Appeal to their interests, invite them, tell them why they will need it in the future and why it will enhance their career goals". It is all about motivation, "Some people need someone to push them".

Q 5 Should IC be assessed?

This question is about if there should be a certificate about IC, and if students would like their IC to be assessed. The immediate answer was "Yes, because I will need it when I apply for a job. Anything that can prove I am competent. A personal statement would be good, like a recommendation from a professor who testifies how you act towards people around you. If it is pleasant to talk to you. Apart from the hard facts and marks just something like 'she functions well'".

Sue added that she studies international communication so "I can show them my degree, but there is no test that can show them if I am competent and I doubt that the company would buy that. You can show them a test about your intercultural competence, but they don't know what that really means".

The group then addressed the difficulties in how IC should be assessed. Grace thinks "it should be part of everybody's education, it is very desirable and possibly having a piece of paper would be useful - if it could be sorted out how to do it."

Kayten mentioned that maybe a situational test would be "better than some test with pass or fail". And it could be combined with an enrichment program. Yousef added that it might "be useful to have people volunteer for some projects or a session like this, then to inform them or give them an email to thank them for their participation. I think a certificate will not be beneficial because everyone can get a certificate".

Maria also believes it is important to get together with people from different parts of the world in workshops and "see if you agree on things, see if you would do things differently, take good ideas forward but not really a test". The recommendation of the group is acknowledgement of participation rather than testing intercultural competence.

Overall, the focus group confirmed the outcome of the student questionnaire. It also, again, showed how close staff and student opinion really is regarding the importance of successful intercultural encounters but also in terms of difficulties in deciding if and how relevant competences should be assessed.

CHAPTER FOUR:

INTERCULTURAL COMMUNICATION AND THE INTERNAL DIVERSITY OF INTELLIGENCES

"Oh, I see," said the Tin Woodman. "But, after all, brains are not the best things in the world."

"Have you any?" enquired the Scarecrow.

"No, my head is quite empty," answered the Woodman; "but once I had brains, and a heart also; so, having tried them both, I should much rather have a heart."

—L. Frank Baum, *The Wonderful Wizard of OZ*, 1900

Towards Successful Communication: A Brief Outline of Concepts and Models

The field of intercultural communication came into being with E.T. Hall's book *The Silent Language*, published in 1959. Research around intercultural competence has also evolved during the last 50 years. Early research was done by Westerners working abroad, in peace corps or as missionaries, who experienced communication problems that affected their work with individuals from different cultural and linguistic backgrounds. Later, in the 1970s and 1980s, intercultural competence research included the experiences of international students, international business relations, expatriates, as well as issues around cultural transition and immigrant acculturation.

In his paper *Exploring and Assessing Intercultural Competence,* Fantini (2006, p. 12) includes a list that reflects the variety of terms that have been used to define intercultural competence, depending on the academic discipline the concept originated from (e.g. linguistics, communications, psychology, ethnology, sociology, business studies, and anthropology): cross-cultural awareness, global competitive intelligence, cultural competence, cultural sensitivity, ethno-relativity, international competence, intercultural interaction, biculturalism, and multiculturalism. Cross-cultural adaptation which focuses on immigrant acculturation, and transcultural communication have also been used by researchers and theorists in this field. As Fantini points out (p.12)

> Some of these stress global knowledge, others sensitivity, still others point to certain skills. (…) most existing terms, definitions, and concepts in use do not adequately capture all that occurs when individuals engage in intercultural contact. Lacking any unifying concept, it is not surprising, therefore, that so many different instruments are being created to measure its outcomes. But the instruments themselves, of course, are only as good as the concepts they attempt to measure.

Fantini describes intercultural competence as "a complex of abilities needed to perform *effectively* and *appropriately* when interacting with others who are linguistically and culturally different from oneself" (p. 13) and emphasises that the notions "effective" and "appropriate" acknowledge both *etic* and *emic* perspectives, that of self (subjective) and other (objective), while also reducing problems of self-report by including the views of both sojourners and hosts regarding outcomes.

The gap between what individuals know about concepts of intercultural competence and what it means to behave in an interculturally competent way, and what those individuals actually do in intercultural situations seems difficult to close (Ruben, 1976; Ruben and Kealey, 1979). In his early framework of intercultural competence, Ruben (1976) presents a behavioural approach to the conceptualization and measurement of intercultural communicative competence which consists of eight dimensions:

- Display of respect (a person's ability to *express respect and positive regard* for another person)
- Interaction posture (a person's ability to *respond to others in a non-judgmental way*)
- Orientation to knowledge (acknowledging that there are different views of the world; the ability to *recognize the extent to which knowledge is individual in nature*)
- Empathy (*ability to put oneself in another's shoes*)
- Task Role Behaviours (ability to *be flexible,* verbal and nonverbal behaviours contributing to group-problem solving activities)
- Relational Role Behaviour (verbal and nonverbal behaviours contributing to building or maintaining relationships in a group, harmonising and mediating to meet the needs and desires of group members
- Interaction management (ability to *take turns in discussion and initiate and terminate interaction; communication skill in governing interactions to meet the needs and desires of group members*)
- Tolerance of ambiguity (a person's ability to *react to new and ambiguous situations with little visible discomfort* (Ruben, 1976).

Later frameworks and models of intercultural competence became more multidimensional and the first comprehensive instruments for measuring cultural competences were developed. In 1992, Bhawuk and Brislin developed their intercultural sensitivity inventory (ICSI) to measure the ability to modify one's behaviour when communicating with people from another culture. Bennett's *Development Model of Intercultural Sensitivity* (DMIS) was based on their concept of intercultural sensitivity and describes (Bennett, 1993) a 6 stage process (denial, defence, minimization, acceptance, adaptation, and integration) leading from an ethnocentric view to an ethnorelative view. Olson and Kroeger (2001) used Bennett's model and developed measuring instruments that represent the six stages of the DMIS as well as the three dimensions of global competency (substantive knowledge, perceptual understanding, and intercultural communication).

A model with a strong focus on communication and interaction was introduced by Byram (1997) in *Teaching and assessing intercultural communicative competence*. In Byram's model, language awareness is central. He focuses on interaction (skills of discovery and interacting) and therefore on a range of communication skills, including verbal and non-verbal communication and the development of linguistic, sociolinguistic, and discourse competencies. Placing these skills in the centre, he proposes a model of intercultural communicative competence that is based on:

- *Attitude* towards self and others (includes "curiosity and openness, readiness to suspend disbelief about other cultures and belief about one's own")
- *Knowledge* of one's self and others (knowing social groups and their practices, both in one's own and in the other culture)
- *skills of interpreting and relating* (to interpret, explain, and relate signs and events from another culture to one's own culture)
- *skills of discovery and interaction* (acquisition of knowledge about another culture and cultural practices; application of existing knowledge and skills in intercultural interactions).
- *critical cultural awareness* (ability to evaluate perspectives, practices and products from different cultural perspectives)

Taking a closer look at ideas that evolved over time around learning and around achieving intercultural competence reveals that the main components seem to be fairly similar. They include attitudes/awareness, knowledge, skills and behaviour (Bloom, 1956; Ting–Toomey, 1993; Byram, 1997; Gudykunst, 1993, 1998; Deardorff, 2004). It is more the shape of the model, the attempt to visualise a rather complex concept and to prioritize some components over others, that reflects the intentions of the researcher and their cultural background. It is not surprising to see a Yin and Yang based model created by a Chinese scholar, or to see foreign language competence as the centrepiece of European models, where different languages are part of everyday life.

Earlier adaptational models (Kim, 1988) and compositional models (Ting-Toomey, 1998, Hamilton et al., 1998) focus on the *components* of intercultural competence, later models include the *process* of intercultural communication. Interestingly, Deardorff (2004) created two models that consist of the same components but still give entirely different impressions of what intercultural competence is really about. Her Pyramid model is compositional and seems to be fixed like a building, a pyramid. The foundation is a large block of attitudes that include respect, openness and curiosity. The next level is marked by knowledge and comprehension that interacts with skills, topped by desired internal outcomes such as an informed frame of reference and finally by desired external outcomes referring to *behaviour*.

The same components set in a model that focuses on the process of interaction is set as a circle of boxes which are connected by arrows of interaction. She is asking the reader to begin with the element of attitude and then work their way around to knowledge and skills, internal and external outcomes. The dynamic of the second model captured my interest in her work and influenced my decision to choose a mechanical device as a visualization tool for the Macquarie model.

Models of intercultural competence are often criticised because they are presented from a Western point of view, though this is not surprising considering that the field of intercultural communication originated in the US and most of the early research around intercultural competence was conducted by Western researchers. There is substantial research for example on Chinese cultural sensitivity (Tjitra and Deng, 2006) as well as Indonesian studies on the topic (Panggabean, 2001), but overall there is a huge gap. Ideally, intercultural competence is a universal key competence, but this might be a Western ideal. Is intercultural competence culture specific after all?

This book presents a study that aims to produce a model of intercultural competence for one single institution, Macquarie University. As Deardorff points out in her introduction to this study, the Macquarie case study reflects "an Australian point of view". Schröder contrasts intercultural competence frameworks in Europe with those developed in Australia and comes to the conclusion that the Europeans follow a more theoretical approach while Australian universities seem to be quicker in implementing theory and embedding intercultural competence into their curricula. On the other hand, Australian society seems to have been less concerned with intercultural skills because it defines itself as a multicultural and open-minded society that may not need additional competences in how to work with people from other parts of the world.

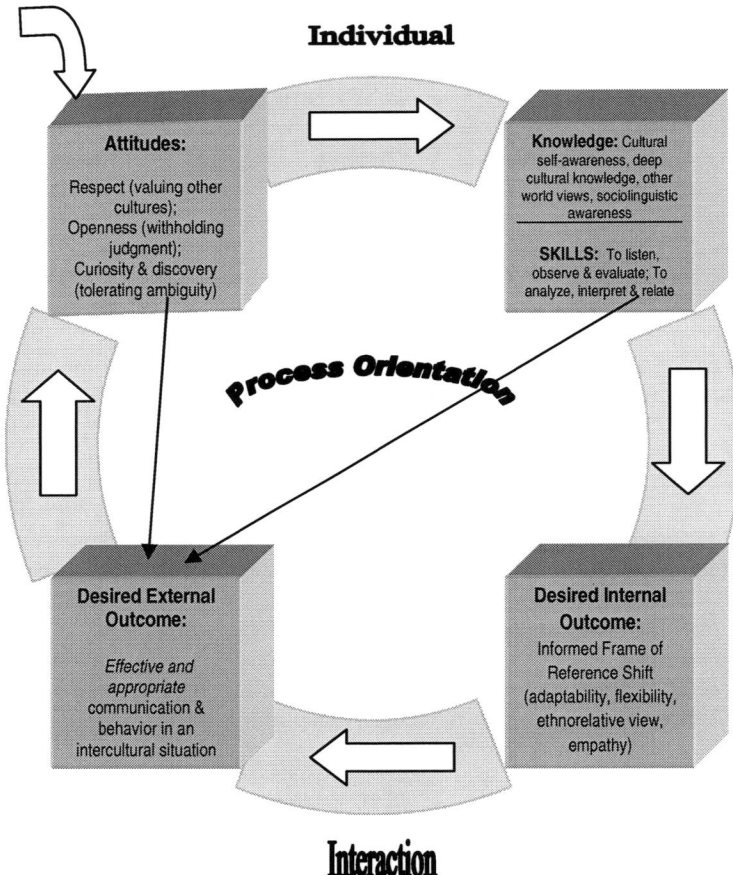

Fig. 1: Intercultural Competence Model (Deardorff, 2006, 2009)

Notes:
- Begin with attitudes: move from individual level (attitudes) to interaction level (outcomes)
- Degree of intercultural competence depends on acquired degree of attitudes, knowledge/comprehension, and skills
  (Diagram and notes printed with permission)

The answer may be just in the use of the terminology: a lot has been said about the shortcomings of concepts such as interculturalism and multiculturalism, mainly because these concepts inherently still assume that there are homogenous and separate single cultures in the world that clash if they share a space and therefore need to meet each other with respect to avoid wars (Welsch, 1999; Kraidy, 2003).

Following Kraidy's argument for critical transculturalism, cultural conditions are largely characterized by mixes and permeations and cultures evolve through borrowing and exchange. This is not a new development since Herder wrote about distinguished folk cultures, but rather the world has always been transcultural and is becoming increasingly so because of continuing globalization processes. Kraidy argues that most analyses of globalization focus on cultural imperialism which influences economic as well as political power and dominance. Studies that focus on processes of hybridization on the other hand, tend to focus on diversity without taking power structures, i.e. shifts in political power, into account. His theoretical framework of critical transculturalism aims to combine these viewpoints by focusing on the hybridizing nature of cultural exchange while paying attention to shifting power distributions and the resulting inequalities. The main concerns of transculturalism are relationships, meaning-making, and power formation (Kraidy, 2005, pp. 9–10)

If hybridity is the logical conclusion of globalization as Kraidy suggests or if at least there is a definite end to separate cultures, a fragmentation of cultures and a range of culture specific models reflecting different parts of the world might be counterproductive to the whole idea of cultural intelligence that leads to *appropriate* behaviour among people from different cultures. As long as globalization reproduces uneven power structures rather than creating a true *third space,* it will be important to have a variety of models of intercultural competence expressing views from different parts of the world.

CULTURAL INTELLIGENCE VS.
INTERCULTURAL COMPETENCE

In psychology, there is no standard definition of what exactly constitutes intelligence; first of all, the concept refers to cognitive abilities and is part of our personality. Rationality, logic and the ability to reason have been explored and attempted to be measured and expressed as a quotient since Spearman (1904) defined cognitive skills as a general, measurable intelligence, referred to as *the g factor*. The quote used as a motto for this chapter is progressive on the one hand because it emphasizes the importance of emotion over that of reason, but it is at the same time stuck in the dichotomy of having to choose between the two. It took almost another century for the Western world to recognise that the concept of general intelligence is too narrow (Sternberg, 1985, 2003; Gardner 1999, 2006), and to acknowledge that people have different kinds of intelligence which complement each other and together form a rounded personality. In African and Asian cultures, intelligence always includes social skills, it includes how one understands and relates to others (Benson, 2003; Yang and Sternberg, 1997). In Western cultures, the importance of emotional intelligence and social skills has been neglected and the focus has instead been on rational decision making (though there were some developments such as Thorndike's notion of *social intelligence* in the 1920s). Emotional Intelligence finally evolved as a Western concept that refers to how one perceives and how one expresses emotions. It is increasingly being recognised as a necessary set of skills that makes people human and functional in a wide range of professions and it is a prime factor in the success of the individual (Goleman, 1995; Matsumoto 1997), in overall performance and in learning.

Emotion display rules, as well as the intensity of emotional expressions, differ across cultures (Matsumoto et al., 1998). In intercultural communication, emotional intelligence therefore needs to include knowledge about these differences across cultures. Even the facial expressions connected to the six emotions that are expressed in a similar way across cultures (Ekmann, 1972, pp. 251-252) are not as universally readable as first assumed: negative emotions such as fear, anger and disgust, for example, are more accurately recognized among Americans than Japanese (Matsumoto, 1991 in Emmerling, R. J. et al, 1999, p. 34). The term "emotional intelligence" (EI) was first defined in 1990 by Salovey and Meyer. Daniel Goleman further developed the concept in his book *Emotional Intelligence* (1995), a concept which is built around understanding oneself and one's own feelings and understanding others and their feelings. The main focus is on mindful communication between people. Goleman identified five areas of emotional intelligence: self-awareness, self-regulation, motivation, empathy and social skills. The range of skills involved can be divided into personal competence (how a person manages him/herself and her own emotions) and social competence (managing relationships, managing the emotions of others). The key word here is awareness. Emotional intelligence has a strong emphasis on awareness and empathy and is therefore indispensable in interpersonal and in particular in intercultural situations. Because of linguistic and cultural difference, there is a high risk of miscommunication and resulting conflict in intercultural communication. Cultural misunderstanding can cause strong emotions like shame or embarrassment and thereby lead to stress which, in turn, will have a negative impact on the relationship of the people involved. The ability to regulate one's own emotions and to recognise and manage emotions in others needs to be included in the set of tools interculturally competent people have at their disposal, as these skills will help to reduce misunderstanding and conflict in intercultural situations.

In recent research that focuses on intercultural issues, the term *cultural intelligence* is replacing that of *emotional intelligence*. The behaviours and attitudes characteristic to emotional intelligence are essential to succeed in developing cultural intelligence. Christopher Earley and Soon Ang (2003) first introduced the term in their book *Cultural Intelligence: Individual Interactions Across Cultures*. Cultural Intelligence (CI) involves knowledge, empathy and self-confidence. Both EI and CI include empathy, understanding the feelings and needs of other people. Cultural intelligence describes self-confidence (self-awareness in EI) as understanding one's own feelings and needs, one's own motivation, strengths and weaknesses, emotional stability and intelligence. Where emotional intelligence stresses awareness and knowledge about one's own emotions and how to regulate them, cultural intelligence includes knowledge about other cultures, people, nations, and behaviours.

As outlined above, CI (Cultural Intelligence) builds on the concepts of IQ (the ability to reason) and EI (Emotional Intelligence) that have been used towards a comprehensive notion of different kinds of intelligence that are complementary. *Cultural Intelligence* refers to the capability to interact effectively across cultures and the term is mainly used in business contexts. Bhawuk et al. (2003, p. 352) acknowledges the similarities between cultural intelligence and intercultural sensitivity and claims that the main difference between the two terms is that CI is *skills oriented* while intercultural sensitivity is a [lifelong learning] *process*.

> Its constant need for commitment and refinement, as well as its fragile and transient nature, require that it be honed and perfected for each encounter. Whereas the skill-based nature of CQ [cultural intelligence] makes it more functional, the process nature of intercultural sensitivity requires more of a commitment to a set way of developing authentic intercultural relationships (p. 352).

This difference may be the reason why *intercultural competence* and *cultural intelligence* are very similar in meaning but used in different contexts. A brief comparison of the two concepts will lead to an understanding of the relevance of cultural intelligence for models of intercultural competence.

Thomas et al. (2008), argue for the use of the term *cultural intelligence* instead of *intercultural competence* and other terms as much more appropriate. They point out some significant differences, such as the nature of *motivation* to act positively toward culturally different others (p. 127). In a business context, the motivation may well be rooted in the desire for personal success rather than in an interest in learning about and accommodating the other. Most of Thomas et al.'s article confirms similarities between the two concepts rather than explicating differences. The most obvious similarity lies, of course, in the goal of culturally intelligent behaviour: just like intercultural competence, cultural intelligence should lead to "more effective intercultural interaction" (p. 125). They see this effective intercultural interaction realized by "good personal adjustment", "the development and maintenance of good interpersonal relationships with culturally different others", and "the effective completion of task-related goals" (p. 125). If we see the completion of task-related goals as skills-oriented, the other criteria are all process-oriented and very close to Deardorff's desired internal outcome (adaptability, flexibility, empathy) and external outcome (effective and appropriate communication and behaviour in an intercultural situation); it is also the same understanding the participants in my study have expressed about what good intercultural communication leads to: effective communication and acceptance of ambiguity, building and maintaining meaningful relationships.

Thomas et al. point out that cultural intelligence is "not static, but involves continuous learning from social interactions" (p. 130). In my Delphi Study, 100% of participants agreed to the notion that "intercultural competence is not static". Regarding personal characteristics and skills that may be indicative of cultural intelligence (and, in comparison, of intercultural competence), Thomas et al. differentiate between personal characteristics, perceptual skills, and relational skills; in the end, these include well known intercultural competencies such as open-mindedness, tolerance of uncertainty and capacity to be non-judgmental. They re-define adaptive skills, such as summarized in Deardorff's internal outcomes. They claim that rather than displaying skills such as self-monitoring, behavioural flexibility and self-regulation, cultural intelligence expresses itself by generating new behaviour that is appropriate to the cross cultural interaction context (p. 130). This idea of creating something new is a reminder of the concept of *third space*, discussed in Chapter One. Regarding this point, the concepts of cultural hybridity, cultural intelligence and critical transculturalism amalgamate.

In intercultural competence models, the "ability to adapt" is a core factor (Gudykunst, 1993, Byram, 1997, Spitzberg, 1997, Deardorff, 2004) and it may refer to the way we communicate as well as to conscious and unconscious mimicry and adaptation to the target culture ("When in Rome, do as the Romans do"). According to Thomas et al., the adaptive behaviour of culturally intelligent people also means shaping the context of the interaction and creating a new environment marked by positive attitudes towards culturally different others. It must be based on the knowledge of culture and on cultural meta-cognition (p. 131) which includes a conscious reflection on and monitoring of available knowledge and skills. It is this definition that Thomas at al. refer to as unique in the concept of *cultural intelligence*, but it is not far from how adaptation is understood in more recent models that focus on *relational* rather than *individual* perspectives towards intercultural competence. The problem here might be the ambiguity of terms such as *adaptability*. In my study, students especially valued *the ability to adapt* (90%), and 73% of the Delphi panel concluded that *the ability to adapt one's own behaviour* is important. What exactly it means to "adapt", or to adapt one's own behaviour, might vary from one person to another and from one situation to another. A relational perspective would locate the ability to adapt in the interaction itself.

Both concepts, cultural intelligence and intercultural competence, have been well defined and their components categorized and related to each other. A startling similarity is that when it comes to measuring the degree of intercultural competence or the progress a person makes in becoming competent, there are few usable guidelines so far and it seems rather difficult to actually use these measuring tools, though in theory they make sense. The main reason for this is that every situation is different, highly context-dependent and subjective. It also remains questionable whether such measuring tools are needed at all. Emmerling and Goleman (2003) address this question of psychological measurement by challenging our attitude towards psychological measurement:

> The use of psychological measurement has always been somewhat controversial, and the measurement of theories within the emotional intelligence paradigm is no different. That the affective experience and abilities of individuals can somehow be quantified has made some uncomfortable. This may, in part, be due to a philosophical view that has seen emotions as unpredictable, irrational, and something to be suppressed in favour of logic and reason. Viewed in this way, emotions and emotional intelligence would hardly be worth measuring even if one could. However, theories of emotional intelligence have helped to counter this view and offered the promise of a more balanced view of what it means to be intelligent about emotions, expanding our understanding of the role that emotions play in mental life (pp. 23/24).

Though there are various comprehensive approaches towards measuring EI (Salovey and Mayer's (1990) approach of measuring emotional intelligence MEIS, and the EQ-i introduced by Bar-On (1997), their reliability and usefulness is still controversial. The same difficulties encountered in measuring emotional intelligence will occur when measuring cultural intelligence; they involve complex subjective processes and a person may do well in one situation but badly in another. In Thomas et al.'s discussion about the implications for measuring cultural intelligence, there are, again, remarkable similarities to the outcome of my study regarding the assessment of intercultural competence: Thomas et al. (p. 136) ascertain that any single approach to measurement of this complex construct is likely to be inadequate and, while it is desirable to arrive at actual behavioural indicators, it seems clear that multiple methods will be required to develop an accurate picture of cultural intelligence. This is also congruent with Deardorff's (2009, p. 486) research result that it is only possible to measure a small number of skills at a time and that assessment of intercultural competence cannot be achieved by relying on one method alone. Thomas et al. conclude their paper by saying that it is particularly difficult to decide on which skills to measure (p. 137) and to avoid cultural bias when developing measuring tools. They therefore leave that task to future researchers.

CHAPTER FIVE:

GOALS OF INTERCULTURAL LEARNING: ACCEPTING AMBIGUITY AND BUILDING MEANINGFUL RELATIONSHIPS

"I spent years trying to figure out how to select people to go overseas. This is the secret. You have to know how to make a friend. And that is it! If you can make friends and if you have a deep need to make friends, you will be successful."
—Edward T. Hall

MEANINGFUL RELATIONSHIPS – THE NOTION OF FRIENDSHIP

The brief comparison between cultural intelligence and intercultural competence in chapter four shows minor differences between the concepts. These are relating to the *motivation* to achieve successful intercultural communication, the *definition* as a tool (cultural intelligence) or a lifelong learning process (intercultural competence), and the nature of the relationship as the most important *outcome*. The term *cultural intelligence* is used mainly in business environments, and the path to successful leadership needs to "link, in managers' minds, the relationship between developing cultural intelligence and success in their future career paths, emphasizing the benefits of learning from different cultures" (Alon and Higgins, 2005, p. 508).

While cultural intelligence in business environments may focus less on harmony and mutual understanding and more on advancing an individual's own career, intercultural competence as a graduate capability of university students aims at both. To "sell" the concept of cultural intelligence or intercultural competence means to develop evidence that respective skills have a positive impact on people's overall performance and leadership potential, and to stress that they are key to personal growth. Business- and success-oriented or not, one of the most important goals is to achieve meaningful relationships. What exactly makes a relationship meaningful, what does the "deep need to make friends" that Hall refers to, mean in times marked by competition and social networking platforms on the internet?

There are views and interpretations of interpersonal relationships and their relevance and meaning for individuals and communities from Aristotle to present day thinkers, but there is little research available about the relationship we call "friendship", especially when it comes to friendship between adults (Allan, 1996, p. 84).

In the Stanford Encyclopedia, Helm (2005) categorizes friendship essentially as a kind of love, a "distinctively personal relationship that is grounded in a concern on the part of each friend for the welfare of the other, for the other's sake, and that involves some degree of intimacy".

Philosophers from the ancient Greeks on have traditionally distinguished three notions that can properly be called love: *agape*, *eros*, and *philia*. *Agape* is a kind of love that does not respond to the antecedent value of its object but instead is thought to *create* value in the beloved; it has come through the Christian tradition to mean the sort of love God has for us persons as well as, by extension, our love for God and our love for humankind in general. By contrast, *eros* and *philia* are generally understood to be responsive to the merits of their objects—to the beloved's properties, especially his goodness or beauty (Helm 2005, p. 2).

Eros has a quality of passion and sexual desire that *philia* does not. Helm comments that *philia* originally meant a kind of affectionate regard or friendly feeling towards not just one's friends but also possibly towards family members, business partners, and one's country at large. C. S. Lewis' short version of the difference between the two, "eros will have naked bodies; friendship naked personalities", suggests a higher level of intimacy and trust than the extended version of *philia* originally had, and therefore declares friendship a much more rare and special bond.

Helm understands friendship as a kind of reciprocated love that involves significant interactions that foster a distinctive kind of intimacy between the friends. Though friendship is a kind of love, Helm (2005, p. 2) points out a vital difference grounded in mutuality: "...whereas we must make conceptual room for the idea of unrequited love, unrequited friendship is senseless".

Friends can be seen as "other selves" (Helm, 2005) and are often described as mirrors of the self, as a projection site for one's own experiences. As C. S. Lewis once put it, "Friendship is born at that moment when one person says to another: 'What! You, too? Thought I was the only one'". But what creates the affective bond that is part of friendship, how do we choose among all the people who could be our friends because of what we value in them, and how do they choose us? The question is if it is our choice at all, or, as Doyle and Smith (2002) suggest in the conclusion of their article about friendship theory, heavily influenced by outer circumstances.

Friendship can be viewed as personal and freely entered into – but it is formed in particular social, economic and cultural circumstances and this has a very significant impact upon the people we meet, and our ability to engage in different activities. It is of profound social as well as individual significance. Through friendship we gain practical and emotional support, and an important contribution to our personal identities. Friendship also helps us to integrate us into the public realm and 'act as a resource for managing some of the mundane and exceptional events' that confront us in our lives. (Allan, 1989, p. 114 in Doyle and Smith, 2002)

Friendship depends on time and place and though it is assumed to be a voluntary, informal and personal relationship, it still operates within the constraints of class, gender, age, ethnicity and geography – and this places a considerable question against the idea that friendship is a matter of choice (Allan, 1989 in Doyle and Smith, 2002).

In times of changing media usage, people talk about their connections through social networking sites as *friends* though they certainly do not have a relationship with all members on their site – most of them would be defined as people they have met at some point, at times only via mediated communication. In terms of degrees of closeness, most of these connections would be acquaintances at best. The casual use of the word "friend" on social networking sites changes the meaning of the term over time. In connection with Facebook, the word friend is also being used as a verb, we hear sentences such as "Tom just friend-ed me on Facebook" or "I'm so going to friend her".

Most languages have ways to express different degrees of friendship, such as "friend", "close friend" and "best friend"; many have completely different words depending on the degree of closeness of the relationship. In languages that use a grammatical polite form for strangers, using the first name only (or a nickname) may be an indication of a closer friendship (Russia, Germany, France). Speakers from these countries will use the term "friend" much more sparsely than, for example, we do in the English language. The word "friend" in English can cover a range of close informal relationships. This means that its use without qualification "can be highly ambiguous" (Pahl, 2000, p.1).

In the context of intercultural communication it may be useful to find common ground on how the notion of friendship can be interpreted across cultural spaces and to have a look at how different languages reflect concepts around friendship. Krappman (1998, p. 24) states that

> ...across all cultures and languages there is a word for a close relationship established outside the narrow family context. (...) We find indications that some languages, during some periods of their development, gave more emphasis to an objective or material reality, such as the importance of mutual help, in close relationships, whereas other languages stressed the affective union of friendship, referring to a subjective reality. (...). The scope of the connotations related to the words used for friendship seems to reflect the socio-historical circumstances under which the friendship was important. The horizon of these meanings includes family issues, ritual

functions, mutual assistance, kindness, war comradeship, conflict solution, intimacy, and affection.

Though there are words reserved for the notion of friendship in all languages, the connotations and derived meanings may differ, even if the etymology is similar. The exact meaning depends on the cultural contexts or socio-historical circumstances Krappman refers to. The status of a friend differs from one culture/language to another. As outlined before, while in some European and Eastern European countries "friend" is only used for a chosen few, in Anglo-Saxon countries people may be called "friends" though there is no close and grown relationship. The basic concept of friendship and its emotional concerns may be quite similar across cultures, though there may be some differences between individualist and collectivist cultures, for example regarding the connection between friendship and society (see Keller, 2004).

Media and mobility have changed environments and means of communication, and thereby also the quantity and possibly the quality or different kinds of connections between people. Societies become more fragmented and family are often not in close proximity, therefore the importance of relationships with friends may increase. However, recent studies show a decline in close friendships in the US, based on interviews that ask about how many people participants can confide in (McPherson, Smith-Lovin, and Brashears, 2006; see also Kornblum, 2006). In light of this development, it will be important to research the values of friendship, the impact of friendship on our personal lives and on social structures across cultures in general.

What does friendship do for us, what is its value for the individual, for a community, and for a society? As a close interpersonal relationship, it has the personal value of constituting and enriching life. Helm (2005) claims that "friendship is undoubtedly central to our lives (...) and our friends can help shape who we are as persons". Friendship has a social value, but in the context of social networking sites it has become a commodity. The values of friendship can be summarised as having the other's interests in mind, feeling for and liking of the other (empathy), and honesty which includes being truthful also in pointing out the other's mistakes. Friends respect each other in their similarities and differences, show mutual understanding and, most of all, they trust in one another which includes being able to show emotions without the fear of being rejected. Friends rely on each other for emotional support.

Friendship is a relationship built upon the whole person and aims at a
psychological intimacy, which in this limited form makes it, in practice, a

rare phenomenon, even though it may be more widely desired. It is a relationship based on freedom and is, at the same time, a guarantor of freedom. A society in which this kind of relationship is growing and flourishing is qualitatively different from a society based on the culturally reinforced norms of kinship and institutional roles and behaviour (Pahl, 2000, pp. 163-4)

Various studies have found links between friendship and health, indicating that strong social support protects people from illness while loneliness may damage physical and mental health (Giles et al., 2005; Helman, 2007). However, there is no proof of a causal link between health and having social support, or that social support in the form of friends prompts us to live healthier lives. Pahl (2000, p. 148) commented:

> It is not friendship *per se* that is important, but rather the trust, security, feelings of self-esteem and feelings of being loved for one's own sake that flow from it.

If friendship and support are vital to emotional wellbeing, it will be crucial for international students and all other sojourners to make friends in the new environment. In their article on transnational education, Kell and Vogl (2008, p. 26) stress the importance of friendship for international students to survive in a foreign environment and they ask "how in the context of the social and structural patterns that promote competition and social fragmentation do people associate and become 'friends'?". Friendship may be changing, and the way forward may be "the development of identity sharing partnerships that are personally liberating and that have a de-institutionalised quality, thereby overcoming the barriers to friendship that include imbalances of power owing to class as well as the 'anxious self'" (Pahl 1998 in Kell and Vogl, 2008). Friendships may be a means of survival for international students, but beyond that immediate gratification they offer the possibility of personal growth and continuous learning, for anyone involved. Friends may be the critical mirror of ourselves, and we learn from them as well as through them. It is this learning process that makes intercultural competence a most important graduate capability for students all over the world. When Kealey and Ruben described the ideal expatriate in 1983, they also defined the ideal friend:

> . . . an individual who is truly open to and interested in other people and their ideas, capable of building relationships of trust among people. He or she is sensitive to the feelings and thoughts of another, expresses respect and positive regard for others, and is non-judgmental. Finally, he or she

tends to be self-confident, is able to take initiative, is calm in situations of frustration and of ambiguity, and is not rigid (p. 165).

They added that "The individual also is a technically or professionally competent person", which emphasises that the important capacity a successful expatriate will have is not her or his professional qualification, but the ability and motivation to build and maintain friendships.

MACQUARIE MODEL
OF INTERCULTURAL COMPETENCE

The most important outcome of this study is that staff and student participants at Macquarie agreed on the nature and the most important goals of intercultural competence, most importantly building and maintaining meaningful relationships. Successful communication is all about relationships, and meaningful relationships can be anything from fruitful business connections that enhance personal success or deep personal connections with someone from a different cultural background. Intercultural communication does include a range of so-called soft skills and knowledge that can be acquired over time, but there is nothing straightforward, romantic or soft about intercultural competence. It is, after all, a vital part of soft power. The vast body of scholarly research that has emerged in the last decades shows just how much hard work it takes to acquire some level of intercultural competence, to teach relevant skills, or to try to measure a person's ability to successfully communicate in intercultural settings.

The final outcomes of the Delphi rounds together with the results of the student survey—both of which have been evaluated by the two external experts, Dr. Darla Deardorff and Prof. Dr Hartmut Schröder—have enabled the determination of a Macquarie model of intercultural competence, along with recommendations for teaching and learning.

Initially I envisioned a model of intercultural competence that is flexible and organic, something that grows naturally and, like a tree, can be pruned, trimmed and fertilized to reach the desired result. However, intercultural competence is not part of nature, it is constructed and often romanticized by visions of equality, understanding and harmony among all people in this world. The results of this research project confirm that successful intercultural communication is key to the development of mutual understanding, but this does not mean that successful communication completely avoids conflict. Societies and individuals will always express difference and need to learn to live with ambiguity and levels of conflict by accumulating the skills to mediate in conflict situations and to form and maintain meaningful relationships.

Kraidy (2005) criticizes studies that celebrate hybridization as a form of diversity while ignoring the power structures involved; it would be equally incomplete to view intercultural competence as the soft skill key to equality and peace while ignoring the concept of power. The notion of power is often invisible in intercultural competence models or in writings about what intercultural competence actually is, but power relations are always present and often an obstacle in attaining and maintaining intercultural skills. Power needs to be part of intercultural communication theory (Gudykunst, 2003, p.185) and needs to be considered a vital factor of intercultural encounters. I have therefore created a rather mechanical model of intercultural competence which comprises a power transmission device with at least three toothed wheels. Rather than part of the visual presentation itself, power is a component of each wheel, it is, for example, part of our linguistic abilities. If we speak the language of the dominant group, we have power; if we share a language with a large group, we also have power; if we speak different languages, our power grows exponentially. Power as social capital is related to social status, nationality, group size, knowledge, communication skills and to connections we already have. New relationships, friendships in particular, will empower the individual and an institution needs to provide mechanisms to steer power and to distribute it in anti-hegemonic and anti-imperialistic ways.

Unlike existing compositional models (Hamilton et al., 1998, Ting-Toomey and Kurogi, 1998, Deardorff's Pyramid model, 2006), or adaptational models (Kim, 1988), the Macquarie model is *process oriented* (like Deardorff's Process model, 2006). The biggest wheel is the *attitude and motivation* wheel, it sets the other two wheels, *knowledge and skills* and *behaviour and outcome*, in motion. I see intercultural competence as an uphill struggle; therefore the big wheel turns the smaller ones for power. Of course, any of the wheels will move the others when set in motion, they are interdependent and they have to work together.

Attitude and motivation: openness, respect, curiosity (about other cultures).

Knowledge and skills: awareness of own culture, culture-specific knowledge, listening skills/communication skills, foreign language skills, ability to adapt, empathy.

Behaviour and outcome: Effective and appropriate communications, ability to accept ambiguity, understanding, build and maintain relationships.

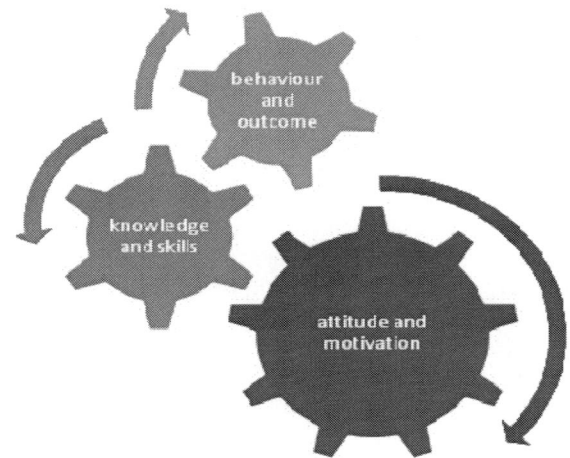

Fig. 5-1 MQ university model of intercultural competence 1

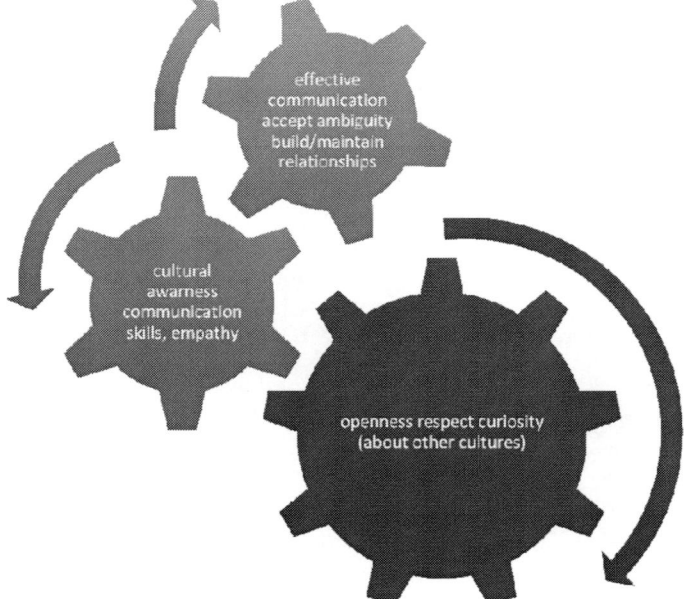

Fig. 5-2 MQ university model of intercultural competence 2

Based on the results of the Delphi Study and the student survey, a working definition of intercultural competence at Macquarie University may be formulated in the following way:

> Intercultural competence means to be open-minded and respectful and to accept ambiguity in all discourse with people, to consider other people's perspectives, and to constantly work towards effective and appropriate communication in order to build and maintain meaningful relationships.

Many of the components in the MQ model are similar to those of current models, but there is special emphasis on building and maintaining relationships, that has evolved as one of the most important outcomes. It is this outcome that distinguishes the MQ model from others and makes it especially suitable in a university context. The literature revisited in this book reflects the need for humans to build close relationships that give meaning to individual lives, it shows concern where meaningful relationships seem to dwindle in times of social networking where everyone seems to compete for the highest number of friends but has no one to trust in; it characterises friendship as one of the most important shapes in our lives; this project, too has shown that students are aware of the number, but more so of the quality of the friendships that they have. Openness and trust, vital elements of friendship, are present in all models of intercultural competence and cultural intelligence. It seems that the true aim of being interculturally competent is to care for the other so as to establish a lasting relationship that involves mutual concern and mutual trust. The wheels of the MQ model turn in different directions and theoretically it does not matter which one is moved first, the components are interconnected and rely on each other to create a whole movement. It also has endless capacity for additional wheels, big and small, that can be integrated into the machine. Most importantly though, the transmission model of intercultural competence relies on people to set it in motion.

SUPPORTING INTERCULTURAL LEARNING

Intercultural competence can be a tool that empowers individuals to successfully relate to others. Language proficiency is undeniably a prerequisite to get in touch with other people and to be able to communicate, and ideally foreign language competence is paired with elements of cultural competence. In fact, without language proficiency, it may not be possible to fully understand a culture and therefore to develop cultural competence (Byram, 1997; Alon and Higgins, 2005). Assuming that language and culture are constituents of each other, teaching and learning foreign languages will always include teaching and learning about culture, and becoming interculturally competent will include some knowledge of other languages. Alon and Higgins point out that the relationship between linguistic competency and cultural intelligence was suggested by Earley & Ang (2003), but needs reinforcement because "Language provides the basis for cultural understanding, intercultural communication, and possible immersion in a foreign culture" (p. 508).

Intercultural skills need to be flexible and ever changing because intercultural communication processes are influenced by a variety of determining factors that impact on identities and patterns of communication. Intercultural competence should be a concern to everyone; it is a steady process of overcoming ethnocentricity and prejudice. My research emphasizes that intercultural education does not concentrate on knowledge transfer alone but needs to constantly work on awareness of the self and the other. Interculturally competent people do not discriminate against but respect the other's identity and though most people know that in theory, they encounter difficulties in everyday life when putting this knowledge into practice. The internationalization survey included in this study reflects how intercultural learning enhances personal and professional growth, but it very much depends on a supportive environment and resources available to students and staff.

Developing intercultural competence can be part of any university subject but needs some intervention and guidance to be successful. Previous studies show that it is not enough to simply rely on culturally diverse groups teaching each other, but that teacher intervention needs to facilitate that learning process (Volet and Ang, 1998). Macquarie provides a rich intercultural context, as well as clear internationalization strategies;

these need to be combined with sustainable strategies and practices that guide intercultural communication and develop intercultural competence. In a linguistically and culturally diverse classroom, different learning styles need to be catered to and a variety of tasks need to be offered that build intercultural competence. The focus group included in this study, for instance, was seen as part of intercultural learning by all participants (including myself) because it was a reflective process of all involved. While it is useful for students to work in culturally and linguistically mixed groups within the classroom, for example on presentations or in guided group discussions, it is vital to include some experiential learning that reaches beyond the classroom and into the wider community.

Universities increasingly introduce schemes and programs that incorporate teaching and learning of intercultural communication skills. Macquarie International, for example, offers the Global Leadership Program to undergraduate and graduate students from across faculties; students participate in this program in addition to their studies and acquire points by choosing from options such as to study or work abroad, complete a cross-cultural practicum, participate in think tanks about global issues, and attend the 'distinguished speaker series'. As of 2012, a range of participation units (PACE) to choose from will be introduced as a compulsory component of most undergraduate degrees. These units are characterized by experiential learning within Sydney, across Australia and abroad. There is, however, a need to introduce and publicise more opportunities and networks for intercultural learning on a day to day basis.

Re-examining the pre Delphi survey, the 3-round Delphi study, and the outcome of the student survey, the following items emerge as indispensable to intercultural learning and should be offered and supported across faculties by institutes of higher education:

- Continuous discipline-specific language support
  o As discussed above, European models focus on language and foreign language proficiency as a core of intercultural competence. In my project, the MQ panel as well as participating students point out that language support, and in particular discipline-specific language support, is indispensable for the community to interact and create real understanding.
  o For domestic students, foreign language learning includes learning about other cultures and points of view. It also creates an awareness of how difficult it is to express one's ideas in another language.

- Intercultural training for lecturers and supervisors (including training in culture-fair grading)
  o Award winning research projects such as *Development and evaluation of resources to enhance skills in higher degree research supervision in a cross-cultural context* offer excellent resources (*The cross cultural supervision project: web-based resources for candidates, supervisors & institutions*) and make them accessible to staff. Research team members are from different Australian universities (Macquarie University, University of Queensland, University of Newcastle 2009)

- Ongoing research in intercultural education, focusing on policies, processes and practices that influence educators and students
  o Universities have taken on the role of preparing their graduates for international careers; many declare intercultural knowledge and competence as a graduate capability for students of all disciplines but this needs to be clearly defined.
  o Research in intercultural education has long been established, but the various projects need to be better linked and publicised.

- Intercultural skills for domestic students
  o Intercultural skills are as important for domestic students as they are for international students who live in multicultural Australia. In my project, domestic students were proportionally underrepresented; those who did participate had been abroad and spoke languages other than English.
  o Domestic students seem to be less aware of and less concerned about intercultural communication issues than international students.

- Intercultural team work
  o Students need more support than the opportunity to learn in culturally diverse classrooms. Intercultural team work in the classroom and within the community needs to be guided to reach learning outcomes beyond the project itself.

- Support materials for teaching development of Intercultural Competence
  Intercultural competence training can be incorporated in units across disciplines, departments and faculties. More resources and

appropriate materials will facilitate its implementation into various subjects and unit designs.

- Curriculum design for intercultural teaching
  o Most university staff cater to diverse student groups and have their international participants in mind when they design courses, assignments or websites. A regular exchange about how to integrate intercultural issues into all units will increase awareness and enhance existing curricula.

- Intercultural training for administrative staff
  o Administrative staff involved in information and admissions, as well as departmental assistants, are often the first contact points for students. They are expected to work with people from all corners of the world, but usually receive no support or training; instead, they are supposed to "learn by doing".
  o Workshops that create awareness and provide a forum for exchange on intercultural skills have been introduced at some institutions of higher education.

- International experience for students and staff (short and long term)
  o International exchange programs for students and staff are crucial for the development of intercultural knowledge. The pre-survey to this study shows that there is a strong emphasis on these programs in fostering intercultural competence.
  o The introduction of participation units at MQ (compulsory from 2012) ensures the inclusion of experiential learning that links theoretical knowledge with practical experience in communities.

- Preparation for staff and students heading into another culture (briefing and de-briefing)
  o It is vital to prepare people for an extended stay abroad via intercultural training. Universities have their own experts who could take up the role of intercultural trainers for specific countries but also in providing general preparation and awareness training.
  o Debriefing will be as important as the preparation and returnees may be able to inform a new group leaving for the same destination of their experiences and give them valuable advice.

- Guest speakers
o Guest speakers have been suggested by the Delphi panel to reach a continuous level of awareness by introducing different perspectives of scholars and practitioners from relevant areas. The possibilities here are endless.

Intercultural learning creates a new way of experiencing one's self and offers the challenge to create new relationships. It allows us to get to know our identities and to express them constitutes our experiences of self and other. We have most in common with people from our own culture and find it easier to communicate with them, but experiencing a new culture may allow different forms of communication and new ways of relating to others. Our identities will change because of the different ways in which we see ourselves and because of the way others perceive us and communicate with us. Even if the impact on our identities is a factor that may be disturbing and frightening at first, it may also be a source of better self-knowledge and of power expressed in additional communicative resources and new relationships that create a wider sense of belonging.

REFERENCES

Adler, P. S. 1975, "The transitional experience: An alternative view of culture shock." *Journal of Humanistic Psychology*, 15(4), 13-23.

Allan, G. 1996, *Kinship and Friendship in Modern Britain*. Oxford: Oxford University Press.

Alon & Higgins 2005, "Global leadership success through emotional and cultural intelligences." *Business Horizons* (48), 501-512.

Anderson, L. E. 1994, "A new look at an old construct: Cross-cultural Adaptation." *International Journal of Intercultural Relations*, 18(3), 293-328.

Bauman, Z. 1997, *Postmodernity and its discontents*. New York: New York University Press.

Bennett, M.J. 1993, Towards Ethnorelativism: A Development Model of Intercultural Sensitivity. In Paige R. M (Ed.) *Education for the intercultural Experience*. Yarmouth, Me: Intercultural Press, 21-71.

Benson, E. 2003, "Intelligence across cultures." *Monitor on Psychology*. February 2003, (34) 2.

Bhabha, H.K. 1994, *The Location of Culture*. London: Routledge.

Bhawuk, D.P.S., & R. Brislin. 1992, "The Measurement of intercultural sensitivity using the concepts of individualism and collectivism." *International Journal of Intercultural Relations*, 16, 413-436.

Bhawuk, D.P.S., Sakuda, K.H., Munusamy, V.P. 2003, Intercultural competence Development and Triple-Loop cultural Learning: Toward a Theory of Intercultural Sensitivity. In Ang, S. van Dyne, L. (eds.) *Handbook of Cultural Intelligence: Theory, Measurement and Application*. P. 242-256.

Bordieu, P. 1973, Cultural Reproduction and Social Reproduction. In Brown R. (Ed.) *Knowledge, Education and Cultural Change*. London: Tavistock.

Bowen, C. Feb 2011, Multiculturalism in the Australian context. http://www.thesydneyinstitute.com.au/podcast/multiculturalism-in-the-australian-context/ Accessed April 4, 2011.

Byram, M. 1997, *Teaching and Assessing Intercultural Communicative Competence*. Clevedon: Multilingual Matters.

Casmir, F. L. 1993, "Third-culture building: A paradigm shift for international and intercultural communication." *Communication Yearbook*. 16, pp. 407-428.

Castells, M. 1997, *The Power of Identity. The information age – economy, society, and culture*. London: Blackwell.

Homewood, Judy, Anna Reid et al. 2009, Cross cultural supervision Project. Available from: http://www.altcexchange.edu.au/group/cross-cultural-supervision-project

Deardorff, D. K. 2006, "Identification and Assessment of Intercultural Competence as a Student Outcome of Internationalization." *Journal of Studies in International Education*, Sept. 01, 10: 241-266.

—. (ed.) 2009, *The Sage Handbook of Intercultural Competence*. Los Angeles, London, New Delhi: Sage.

Dalkey, N. C. 1972, The Delphi method: an experimental application of group opinion. In N. C. Dalkey, D. L. Rourke, R. Lewis, & D. Snyder (eds.) *Studies in the quality of life*. Lexington, MA: Lexington Books.

Delbecq, A. L., Gustafson, D. H. & Van de Ven, A. H. 1975, *Group Techniques for Program Planning: A guide to nominal group and Delphi processes*. Management Application Series, Glenview, Ill: Scott, Foresman and Co.

Doyle, M. E. & Smith, M. K. 2002, "Friendship: theory and experience", *The encyclopaedia of informal education*. Available from http://www.infed.org/biblio/friendship.htm

Dunn, K.M., Klocker, N. & Salabay, T. 2007, Contemporary racism and Islamaphobia in Australia: racialising religion." Ethnicities, 7(4), 564-589.

Dunn, K.M. Inaugural Professorial lecture. Available from: http://www.uws.edu.au/arts/coa/professorial_lecture_series/prof_kevin_dunn

Ekman, P. 1972, Universals and Cultural Differences in Facial Expressions of Emotion. In J. Cole (Ed.), Nebraska Symposium on Motivation (Vol. 19, pp.207-282). University of Nebraska Press.

Emmerling, R. J. & Goleman, D. 2003, "Emotional intelligence: Issues and common misunderstandings". *Issues and Recent Developments in Emotional Intelligence* 1(1), Retrieved April 22, 2011, from http://www.eiconsortium.org

Fantini, A.E. (Ed.) 1997, *New ways of teaching culture*. Alexandria, Va.: TESOL.

Fantini, A.E. & Tirmizi, A. 2006, "Exploring and Assessing Intercultural Competence" *World Learning Publications*. Paper 1. Retrieved April 20, 2011 http://digitalcollections.sit.edu/worldlearning_publications/1

Featherstone, M. 1990, Global Culture. An Introduction. In *Theory, Culture & Society*, vol. 7, pp. 1-14.

French, W. L. & Bell C. H. 1979, *Organizational Development*. New Jersey: Prentice Hall.

Friedman, J. 1994, *Cultural Identity and Global Process*. London: Sage.

Gardner, H. 1999, *Intelligence Reframed. Multiple intelligences for the 21st century*, New York: Basic Books.

Gardner, H. 2006, *Changing Minds. The art and science of changing our own and other people's minds*. Boston MA.: Harvard Business School Press.

Giles, L., Glonek, G., Luszcz, M.A., Andrews, G.A. 2005, "Effect of social networks on 10 year survival in very old Australians: the Australian longitudinal study of aging". *Journal of Epidemiology & Community Health* 2005; 59: 574-579.

Giles, C. L., Glonek, F. V. G., Luszcz, A. M., & Andrews, R. G. 2005, "Effects of social networks on 10 year survival in very old Australians: the Australian longitudinal study of aging". *Journal of Epidemiology Health*, 59, 574-579.

Goleman, D 1995, *Emotional intelligence: why it can matter more than IQ*. New York: Bantam Books.

—. 1996, *Emotionale Intelligenz*. München: Hanser-Verlag.

Gudykunst, W.B. & Ting-Toomey, S. 1988, *Culture and Interpersonal Communication*. Californina State University, Fullerton: Sage.

Gudykunst, W.B. 1991, *Bridging Differences: Effective Intergroup Communication*. Newbury Park, Ca: Sage.

Gudykunst, W. B. & Kim, Y. Y. 1992, *Communicating with Strangers*. New York: McGraw Hill, Inc.

Gudykunst, W. B. 1993, Toward a theory of effective interpersonal and intergroup communication. In Wiseman, R.J. and Koester, J. (Eds.), *Intercultural communication competence* (International and Intercultural Communication Annual, Vol. 16, pp. 3–71). Newbury Park, CA: Sage.

—. 2003, Intercultural Communication Theories. In

—. (ed) *Cross-cultural and intercultural communication*. Thousand Oaks, Ca.: Sage.

Guibernau, M., & Rex, J. (eds.) 2010, *The Ethnicity Reader: Nationalism, Multiculturalism and Migration*. Cambridge: Polity Press.

Hall, E.T. 1959, 1973, *The Silent Language*. New York: Anchor Books

—. 1976, *Beyond Culture*. New York: Doubleday.

Hartup, W. & Stevens, N. 1997, "Friendships and Adaptation in the Life Course". *Psychological Bulletin,* 121(3), 355-370.

Helm, B.W. 2009, *Love, Friendship, and the Self. Intimate Identification and the Sociality of Persons*. New York, Oxford: Oxford University Press.

—. 2005, Love. In Zalta, E.N (Ed.) *The Stanford Encyclopedia of Philosophy*. Available from: http://plato.stanford.edu/entries/friendship/

Helman, Cecil G 2007(5th ed), *Culture, Health and Illness*. London: Hodder Arnold.

Helmer O. 1983, *Looking Forward: A Guide to Futures Research*. Beverly Hills: Sage.

Hofsteede, G. 1991, *Cultures and Organizations: Software of the Mind*. New York: McGraw-Hill.

Howes, D. (ed.) 1996, *Cross-Cultural Consumption: Global Markets, Local Realities*. London, New York: Routledge.

Hymes, D.H. 1972, On Communicative Competence. In J.B. Pride and J. Holmes (eds) *Sociolinguistics. Selected Readings*. Harmondsworth: Penguin, 269-293.

Jandt, F. 1995, *Intercultural Communication - An Introduction*. Thousand Oaks: Sage.

Kealey, D. J., & Ruben, B. D. 1983, Cross-cultural personnel selection: Criteria, issues and methods. In D. Landis & R. W. Brislin (Eds.), *Handbook of intercultural training* (1), 155–175). New York: Pergamon.

Keller, M. 2005, "A Cross-Cultural Perspective on Friendship Research". *ISBBD Newsletter, 46*(2),10–11, 14. Max Planck Institute for Human Development, Berlin

Kell, P.M. & Vogl, G. 2008, "Trans-national education: The politics of mobility, migration and the wellbeing of international students." *International Journal of Asia Pacific Studies*, May 2008, *4*,(1): 21-31.

Kim, Y. 1988, *Communication and cross-cultural adaptation: An integrative theory*. Philadelphia: Multi-Lingual Matters.

—. 2009, The Identity Factor in Intercultural Competence. In D. K. Deardorff (ed.) *The Sage Handbook of Intercultural Competence*. Los Angeles, London, New Delhi: Sage.

Kornblum, J. 2006, June 22, Study: 25% of Americans have no one to confide in. *USA Today*. Retrieved from http://www.usatoday.com/news/nation/2006-06-22-friendship_x.htm)

Kraidy, M. 2005, *Hybidity or the Cultural Logic of Globalization*. Philadelphia: Temple University Press.

Krajewski, S. & Schröder, H. 2008, Silence and Taboo. In G. Antos and E. Ventola (eds.) *Handbook of Interpersonal Communication.* Berlin, New York: Mouton de Gruyter 2008, 595-619.

Krajewski, S. (2011) "Teaching intercultural communication in multicultural and multilingual groups." *Journal of Research in International Education* (10)2, Sage.

Kramsch, C. 1993, *Context and culture in language education,* Oxford: Oxford University Press.

Krappman, L. 1998, Amicita, drujba, shin-yu, philia, freundschaft, friendship: On the cultural diversity of a human relationship. In Bukowski, W.M, Newcomb, A.F, Hartup, W.W. (eds.) *The Company They Keep. Friendships in Childhood and Adolescence.* Cambridge Studies in Social and Emotional Development, Cambridge University Press, 19-40.

Lewis, C.S. 2002, *The Four Loves.* London: Harper Collins, 78-9.

Linstone, H. A. & Turoff, M. (eds.) 1975, *The Delphi Method: Techniques and applications.* Reading, Mass.: Addison-Wesley Publishing Company.

Matsumoto, D. 1990, "Cultural similarities and differences in display rules." *Motivation & Emotion, 14,* 195-214.

—. 1991, "Cultural Influences on facial expressions of emotion." *Southern Communication Journal,* 56, 128-137.

Matsumoto, D., Takeuchi, S., Andayani, S., Kouznetsova, N., and Krupp, D. 1998, "The contribution of individualism-collectivism to cross-national differences in display rules." *Asian Journal of Social Psychology,* 1, 147-165.

McAllister, L., Whiteford, G., Hill, R Thomas, N & M. Fitzgerald 2006, "Reflection in intercultural learning: Examining the international experience through a critical incident approach". *Journal of Reflective Practice Vol. 7, 3, 367–381.*

McPherson, M. Smith-Lovin, L., Brashears, M.E. 2006, "Social Isolation in America: Changes in Core Discussion Networks over Two Decades." *American Sociological Review,*71(3), 353-375.

Merkel says German multicultural society has failed. BBC News 17/10/10. Available from: http://www.bbc.co.uk/news/world-europe-11559451

Oberg, K. I960, "Culture shock: Adjustment to new cultural Environments." *Practical Anthropology,* 7, 177-182.

Olson, C. L., & Kroeger, K. R. 2001, "Global competency and Inter-cultural sensitivity." *Journal of Studies in International Education,* 5, 116-137.

Pahl, R. 1998, Friendship: The Social Glue of Contemporary Society? In J. Franklin (ed.) The Politics of Risk Society, 99-119. Cambridge: Polity Press.

—. 2000, *On Friendship*. Oxford: Polity Press.

Paige, R.M. 1990, International students: Cross-cultural psychological Perspectives. In R. W. Brislin (Ed.), *Applied cross-cultural psychology*, 161-185, Newbury Park, CA: Sage.

Paige, R.M, Jorstad, H., Siaya, L., Klein, F., & Colby, J. 2003, Culture learning in language education: A review of the literature. In D. Lange & R.M. Paige (Eds.), *Culture as the core: Integrating culture into language education*. Greenwich, CT: Information Age Publishing, 173-236.

Palmer, B. R., Gignac, G., Ekermans, G. and Stough, C. 2008, A Comprehensive Framework for Emotional Intelligence. In Emmerling, R.J. Shanwal, V.K., Mandal, M.K.(eds.) *Emotional Intelligence: Theoretical and Cultural Perspectives*. NY: Nova Publishers, 17 – 38.

Panggabean, H. 2001, *Characteristics of intercultural sensitivity in Indonesian-German work groups*. Unpublished doctoral dissertation, University of Regensburg, Germany.

Paquet, G. 2008, *Deep Cultural Diversity. A Governance Challenge*. Ottawa: University of Ottawa Press.

Parker, R Stephen, Haytko, Diana L, Hermans, Charles M. 2009, "Individualism and Collectivism: Reconsidering old assumptions." *Journal of International Business Research*.

Prechtl, E. & Lund, A. D. 2007, Intercultural competence and assessment: Perspectives from the INCA Project. In Helga Kotthoff & Helen Spencer-Oatey (eds). *Handbook of Intercultural Communication*. Berlin: Mouton de Gruyter.

Rex, J. 2010, The concept of a Multicultural Society. In Guibernau, M., and Rex, J. (eds.) *The Ethnicity Reader: Nationalism, Multiculturalism and Migration*. Cambridge: Polity Press, 217-229.

Ruben, B. D. 1976, "Assessing communication competency for intercultural adaptation." *Group and Organisation Studies*, (1) 3, 334-354.

Ruben, B. D., & Kealey, D. 1979, "Behavioral assessment of communication competency and the prediction of cross-cultural adaptation." *International Journal of Intercultural Relations, 3*, 15-48.

Salovey, P. & Mayer, J. D. 1990, "Emotional Intelligence." *Imagination, Cognition, and Personality*, 9, 185-211.

Selfridge, R. J. and Sokolik, S. L. 1975, "A Comprehensive View of Organizational Development." *MSU Business Topics*, 47.

Selman, R. L. 1980, *The growth of interpersonal understanding. Developmental and clinical analyses.* New York: Academic Press.

Shannon, C. E. & W. Weaver 1949, *A Mathematical Model of Communication.* Urbana, IL: University of Illinois Press.

Spitzberg, B. H. 1997, Intercultural effectiveness. In L. A. Samovar & R. E. Porter (Eds.) *Intercultural communication: A reader* (8th ed., 379–3391). Belmont, CA: Wadsworth.

Sternberg, R. J. 1985, *Beyond IQ: A triarchic theory of human intelligence.* New York: Cambridge University Press.

Stitt-Gohdes, W. L. & Crews, T. B. 2004, "The Delphi technique: A research strategy for career and technical education." *Journal of Career and Technical Education 20*(2), 53-65.

Syed, J. & Kramar, R. 2010, "What is the Australian model for managing cultural diversity?" *Personnel Review* 39(1), 96-115.

Tjitra, H.W. & Deng, W. 2006, Chinese Intercultural Sensitivity in Contemporary China. In W. Dreyer & U. Hoessler (Eds.). *Perspectives of Intercultural Competence.*

Ting-Toomey, S. 1993, Communicative resourcefulness: An identity negotiation perspective. In R. L. Wiseman, and J. Koester (Eds.), *Intercultural communication theory,* 72-111. Newbury Park, CA: Sage.

—. 1997, Intercultural Conflict Competence. In Cupach, W. and D. Canary (Eds) *Competence in interpersonal Conflict.* New York: McGraw-Hill, 120-147.

Thomas, D. C., Elron, E., Stahl, G., Ekelund, B.Z., Ravlin, E.C., Cerdin, J., Poelmans, S., Brislin, R., Pekerti, A., Aycan, Z., Maznevski, M., Au, K., & Lazarova, M.B. 2008, "Cultural Intelligence: Domain and Assessment." *International Journal of Cross Cultural Management* August, 8(2), 123-14.

Thomas, D.C. & Kerr Inkson 2004, *Cultural Intelligence: People Skills for Global Business.* Berrett-Koehler Publishers, Inc.

Thorndike, R.K. 1920, "Intelligence and Its Uses." *Harper's Magazine* 140, 227-335.

Tomlinson, J. 2003, Globalization and Cultural Identity. In D. Held et al. (eds.). *The Global Transformations Reader* (2nd edition). Cambridge: Polity Press.

Trompenaars, F. & Hampden-Turner, C. 1997, *Riding the Waves of Culture: Understanding Cultural Diversity in Business.* London: Nicholas Brearley.

Vainio, S. 2008, Quality assurance and the role of students within the university community. Available from:
http://www.utu.fi/en/university/quality/students.html

Volet, S. & Ang, G. 1998, "Culturally mixed groups on international campuses: An opportunity for intercultural learning." *Higher Education Research and Development*, 17(1), 5-23.

Welsch, Wolfgang 1999, Transculturality – The puzzling form of cultures Today. In Featherstone, M. and Lash, S. (eds.) *Spaces of Culture: City, Nation, World*. London: Sage, 194-213.

Wood, P. & Landry, C. 2008, *Intercultural City. Planning for diversity advantage*. London: Earthscan.

Yang, S. & Sternberg, R. J. 1997, "Taiwanese Chinese people's conceptions of intelligence." *Intelligence* 25, 21–36.

Appendix A

Internationalization Survey

Apart from generating names for the Delphi study, this survey focused on 6 questions to elicit opinions from the deans, colleagues at MQ International and the Centre for Social Inclusion about relevant issues in the area of intercultural communication and intercultural competence. An open box for additional answers was provided after each set of answer suggestions; multiple answers were allowed. Participants were asked, firstly, "which area of internationalization is especially important to and supported by your faculty?" Answer suggestions in the order of how many participants rated them as important:

- International student programs (10)
- Exchange programs (8)
- Internationalization of research (7)
- International student and community support services (7)
- Internationalization of curriculum (4)
- Internationalization of teaching (3)

In addition, "indigenous exchange esp. Maori and North American" was suggested.

The second question "Where do you see most need for support of internationalization efforts at Macquarie?" was an open question that received 12 answers which have been put into clusters:

Responses re language

- Competence in English/ English language and culture
- Language support

Responses re intercultural competence

- Intercultural competence
- Development of cross-cultural competences in teaching and learning
- Creating awareness amongst domestic students of the importance of their being able to think beyond career and study possibilities in Australia through greater interaction with international students, and by going on exchange and other outbound programs
- Training of lecturers and supervisors
- Mix the intake to achieve a cultural diversity
- Multilateral cross-university joint activity in learning, teaching, research and esp. community engagement.
- Use domestic and international student groups/classes for mutual exchange
- Support with international students with regard to their holistic needs

Other

- Administrative support
- More rooms
- All areas listed in q1

Question number 3 asked "which existing schemes available to staff and students at MQ are most important for internationalization at MQ"?
This question received 11 answers of which 6 referred to international exchange programs for students/staff. Two respondents mentioned MQ International.

Other answers

- Conferences/international conference support, cotutelle (2), curriculum designed to teach intercultural competence, OSP.
- Induction and ongoing support services, affordable housing
- Supervisor training

Asked about in which areas of internationalization respondents see a need for the development of additional schemes for staff and students (question number 4), respondents referred back to Q 2 and 3 and said that there should be more of everything, more joint programs, more housing, more staff exchange. All answers reflected the need of language support and the need to develop intercultural competence in the MQ community.

Areas mentioned again in need of more support were

For staff:
- Support materials for teachers' development of cross-cultural abilities
- Overseas staff exchange and staff development through greater availability of international studies programs. An optional free study component to work would be a good incentive.
- Cultural understanding of home countries
- Culture fair grading

For students:
- Language and cultural understanding
- Coherent discipline-specific language support programs run by people with experience of postgraduate and doctoral programs and with specialist training in designing such courses
- Support for study skills development for overseas students
- Assistance with academic discourse
- Build accommodation into international program

In general:
- Working in diverse teams
- Better developed cultural sensitivity and literacy
- Preparation for all staff and students heading into another culture
- Around social capital

The next two questions referred to the *effect and use of intercultural competence*. Question 5 asked respondents if they thought the wider community would profit from measurable intercultural skills of MQ graduates. Answers ranged from "I don't think the community would be worried by this" to "the community will see MQ as an example of cultural understanding and progress". Two respondents questioned if intercultural skills can or should be measured. Most respondents (10 out of 13) attributed positive effects such as more acceptance and better harmony in the wider community, better prevention and resolution of problems which originate in communication problems between cultures at home, greater success at exporting into other cultures and better engagement with and understanding of intercultural issues by looking at questions from more than one point of view.

Question 6 asked about advantages for MQ graduates who have acquired measurable intercultural skills during their studies. Eleven participants answered, all of them do see advantages, and one person specified that there are possible advantages if these skills include a second or third language.

Indicated advantages for the professional future
- Intercultural teamwork among local and international students benefits local students as it provides them with greater skills for communicating in the workplace with people from different backgrounds
- They are better prepared for careers in a world which increasingly includes intercultural teamwork
- The ability to adapt and improve communication skills through greater understanding of others they work with
- They will be more effective human service workers

...and for personal growth
- Ability to work in teams with members from different nationalities, accents, cultures
- Global citizens able to function effectively wherever they go
- Better engagement with and understanding of intercultural issues, more than one point of view, increased willingness to live and work in other countries
- Ability to think globally

Appendix B

Questionnaires

Internationalisation

The purpose of this project is to create a better understanding of intercultural competence and how it can be developed in our students. The study is being conducted by Dr Sabine Krajewski (Tel: 98502167) of the Centre of International Communication and is supported by a MQ Social Inclusion Grant.

Any information or personal details gathered in the course of this study are confidential.

1.   Is there an area of internationalisation that is especially important to and supported by your faculty?

☐   International student programmes

☐   Internationalisation of teaching

☐   Internationalisation of curriculum

☐   Exchange programmes

☐   Internationalisation of research

☐   International student and community support services

☐   Other, please specify

2. Where do you see most need for support of internationalisation efforts at Macquarie University?

```
┌─────────────────────────────────┐
│                                 │
│                                 │
└─────────────────────────────────┘
```

3. Which existing schemes available to staff and/or students do you consider most important for internationalisation at Macquarie?

```
┌─────────────────────────────────┐
│                                 │
│                                 │
└─────────────────────────────────┘
```

4. In which areas of internationalisation do you see a need for the development of additional schemes for staff and students?

```
┌─────────────────────────────────┐
│                                 │
│                                 │
└─────────────────────────────────┘
```

5. How do you think the wider community will profit from measurable intercultural skills of Macquarie graduates?

```
┌─────────────────────────────────┐
│                                 │
│                                 │
└─────────────────────────────────┘
```

6. Which advantages do you see for Macquarie graduates who have acquired measurable intercultural skills during their studies?

```
┌─────────────────────────────────┐
│                                 │
│                                 │
└─────────────────────────────────┘
```

7. Please name up to 5 people within Macquarie University who have expertise in intercultural communication and/or intercultural competence and might be candidates to participate in this study as part of an expert panel.

IC expertise may be evident through relevant publications, teaching or other work experience in the field, relevant experience abroad, membership in certain committees or other aspects.

1 ☐

2 ☐

3 ☐

4 ☐

5 ☐

8. If there are further questions, may I contact you again in regard to this project?

☐   Yes

☐   No

Thank you very much for your time and your help.

Pre-Delphi survey

1. You have been identified as an expert in the field of intercultural communication and intercultural competence. Please self-assess what makes you an expert:

☐   I have work experience in ICC (outside of the university, eg. as intercultural trainer)

☐   I have teaching experience in ICC

☐   I have published in the field

☐   I have designed teaching material related to intercultural competence

☐   Other (please specify)

2. What is your cultural background?

3. What intercultural knowledge and skills do you think students should develop while studying at MQ?

4. What are the best ways to include intercultural competence in undergraduate and postgraduate curricula at Macquarie University?

5. Do you think students' intercultural competence should be assessed?

□   Yes

□   No

□   Not sure

6. If you think it should be assessed, what is the purpose/use of an ICC assessment?

```
┌─────────────────────────────┐
│                             │
│                             │
└─────────────────────────────┘
```

7. If you decide to participate in the Delphi study, you will be asked to answer 2 open questions in the first Delphi round. In 2 subsequent rounds you will be asked to rank answers on a Likert-type-scale.
The first round may take around half an hour of your time. Subsequent rounds will take approximately 15 minutes each.
Any information or personal details gathered in the course of the study are confidential. No individual will be identified in the publication this study feeds into.

Would you be interested in participating in a 3 round Delphi study about intercultural competence as a member of the expert panel?

□   Yes

□   No

□   Maybe (please specify)

```
┌─────────────────────────────┐
│                             │
│                             │
└─────────────────────────────┘
```

Thank you very much for your time and your help.

Delphi round 1

The aim of this Delphi Study is to reach consensus about what intercultural competence actually is and how it can best be measured. Please give comprehensive answers to the following 2 questions. In subsequent rounds you will be asked to rank answers given by members of the expert panel.

1. What constitutes intercultural competence?

```
┌─────────────────────────────────┐
│                                 │
│                                 │
└─────────────────────────────────┘
```

2. How do you think intercultural competence can best be measured?

```
┌─────────────────────────────────┐
│                                 │
│                                 │
└─────────────────────────────────┘
```

Thank you!

The Student Voice: Questionnaire

You are invited to participate in a study about intercultural competence. This project is being conducted by Dr Sabine Krajewski and Kristina Wolters from the Department of Media, Music, Communication and Cultural Studies. Sabine Krajewski can be contacted via email Sabine.krajewski@mq.edu.au or by phone (98502167).

The purpose of the study is to create a better understanding of intercultural competence and how it can be developed in our students. This project is funded through a Social Inclusion grant from Macquarie University. It will take you about 15 minutes to complete the following questionnaire. You may win one of 4 gift vouchers worth $25 each!

1. What do you think about the following statements:

Please choose an answer that expresses your opinion.

	strongly agree	agree	somewhat agree	somewhat disagree	disagree	strongly disagree
It is important to be able to get along with people from other cultures	□	□	□	□	□	□
Intercultural Competence should be a graduate capability at MQ	□	□	□	□	□	□
Intercultural Competence is only important for people who plan to work in an international environment	□	□	□	□	□	□
Intercultural Competence is an	□	□	□	□	□	□

	strongly agree	agree	somewhat agree	somewhat disagree	disagree	strongly disagree
extra skill that should not be a general graduate capability at MQ						
I would like to have some sort of certificate about my intercultural skills when I graduate	□	□	□	□	□	□
Intercultural skills are important but future employers are not interested in them	□	□	□	□	□	□
I sometimes find it difficult to interact with people from other cultural and linguistic backgrounds	□	□	□	□	□	□
There are already enough programs at MQ about intercultural skills	□	□	□	□	□	□
There is a need for more extracurricular workshops about intercultural competencies	□	□	□	□	□	□

	strongly agree	agree	somewhat agree	somewhat disagree	disagree	strongly disagree
Intercultural competencies should be an integral part of as many classes as possible	☐	☐	☐	☐	☐	☐
Intercultural Competence is more important for international students than for local students	☐	☐	☐	☐	☐	☐
There should be more training for staff about how to cater to internationalised student groups	☐	☐	☐	☐	☐	☐
I would be interested in attending extra-curricular workshops to gain intercultural skills	☐	☐	☐	☐	☐	☐
MQ classes are so diverse that I automatically gain intercultural competence	☐	☐	☐	☐	☐	☐
It is important to know one's own cultural background in	☐	☐	☐	☐	☐	☐

	strongly agree	agree	somewhat agree	somewhat disagree	disagree	strongly disagree
order to have good interaction with students from other cultures						

other (please specify)

```
┌─────────────────────────────┐
│                             │
│                             │
└─────────────────────────────┘
```

2. How important are the following issues when you want to successfully communicate with people from other cultures? Feel free to add other items that you find important when communicating with people from other cultures.

	very important	important	a little bit important	not very important	rather unimportant	not important at all
Communication skills	☐	☐	☐	☐	☐	☐
Foreign language skills	☐	☐	☐	☐	☐	☐
awareness of my own culture	☐	☐	☐	☐	☐	☐
emotional stability	☐	☐	☐	☐	☐	☐

	very important	important	a little bit important	not very important	rather unimportant	not important at all
knowledge of nonverbal language	☐	☐	☐	☐	☐	☐
openness	☐	☐	☐	☐	☐	☐
tolerance	☐	☐	☐	☐	☐	☐
empathy (ability to take the perspective of the other person)	☐	☐	☐	☐	☐	☐
respect	☐	☐	☐	☐	☐	☐
awareness of the language behind the culture	☐	☐	☐	☐	☐	☐
curiosity about (other)cultures	☐	☐	☐	☐	☐	☐
culture-specific knowledge	☐	☐	☐	☐	☐	☐
imagination	☐	☐	☐	☐	☐	☐
listening skills	☐	☐	☐	☐	☐	☐
ability to adapt	☐	☐	☐	☐	☐	☐
flexibility	☐	☐	☐	☐	☐	☐

Other (please specify)

Please finish the following statements:

1. To me, Internationalisation at Macquarie University means

```
┌─────────────────────────────┐
│                             │
│                             │
└─────────────────────────────┘
```

2. I think the most important things about intercultural communication and intercultural competence are

```
┌─────────────────────────────┐
│                             │
│                             │
└─────────────────────────────┘
```

3.   The following questions are about yourself.

         I am

□   male   □   female

4.   I am a

                 undergraduate student   graduate/postgraduate student

1st year   □

2nd year   □

3rd year   □

4th year   □

MA   □

PhD   □

5. Faculty:

```


```

6. Subject:

```


```

7. Cultural background:

```


```

8. Age group

☐   under 20

☐   20-25

☐   25-35

☐   35+

9. Mother tongue:

```


```

10. I also speak

```


```

Thank you very much!

INDEX